RIDING ON THE
WILD SIDE

RIDING ON THE WILD SIDE

Tales of Adventure in the Canadian West

HUMAN INTEREST/ BACKCOUNTRY

by Dale Portman

PUBLISHED BY ALTITUDE PUBLISHING CANADA LTD.
1500 Railway Avenue, Canmore, Alberta T1W 1P6
www.altitudepublishing.com
1-800-957-6888

Extreme care has been taken to ensure that all information presented in
this book is accurate and up to date. Neither the author nor the
publisher can be held responsible for any errors.

Publisher	Stephen Hutchings
Associate Publisher	Kara Turner
Editors	Gayl Veinotte, Kara Turner

We acknowledge the financial support of the Government
of Canada through the Book Publishing Industry Development
Program (BPIDP) for our publishing activities.

Altitude GreenTree Program

Altitude Publishing will plant twice as many trees as were used
in the manufacturing of this product.

National Library of Canada Cataloguing in Publication Data

Portman, Dale
Riding on the wild side / Dale Portman.

(Amazing stories)
Includes bibliographical references.
ISBN 1-55153-985-3

1. Portman, Dale. 2. Park rangers--Rocky Mountains, Canadian (B.C.
and Alta.)--Biography. 3. Horses--Rocky Mountains, Canadian (B.C. and Alta.)
I. Title. II. Series: Amazing stories (Canmore, Alta.)

SB481.6.P67A3 2004   333.78'3'092   C2003-907432-3

An application for the trademark for Amazing Stories™
has been made and the registered trademark is pending.

Printed and bound in Canada by Friesens
2 4 6 8 9 7 5 3 1

Cover: Nothing matches the sheer exhilaration of watching wild horses running free.

Dedicated to the memory of Bert and Faye Mickle,
Keith Foster, Jim Rimmer, Cal Hayes, and Art Twomey,
many of whom passed on much too early in life.

Contents

Ya Ha Tinda Bound

There's a place on the Eastern Slope
In the mountains deep
It's a place of rolling grass
Where the Red Deer River sweeps
I'm riding north into that land
Where silence can be found
I'm riding north, I'm Ya Ha Tinda bound

In Canada the great white north
The bitter cold descends
Alpine passes choke with snow
And Mother Nature sends
A bitter wind down valleys steep
Is running southern bound

These ponies they deserve a rest
Been goin' hard since June
Step out son it's not far now
We're gonna be there soon
These horses tend to slip and slide
And skid on frozen ground
I'm riding north, I'm Ya Ha Tinda bound

When I arrive, I'll pull their shoes
And turn 'em out on grass
They will lope out through the gate
They are free at last
When heavy snows obscure the ground

Ya Ha Tinda Bound

They'll feed on bales round
I'm riding north, I'm Ya Ha Tinda bound

I see the ranch past Warden Rock
As vistas open wide
My pace picks up this is the end
Of a long and cold hard ride
When spring arrives, we'll chase 'em in
And trail them to town
Then after six months work, they'll be Ya Ha Tinda bound

John and Dick and Rob they train
The colts from good ranch stock
They'll gentle 'em and ride 'em hard
'Til they don't shy or balk
And when those colts go to the parks
They'll be good and sound
And after six months work, they'll be Ya Ha Tinda bound

And when I'm old and crippled up
And can no longer ride
I will sit out on my porch and remember vistas wide
And when its time to bury me
Beneath the cold hard ground
In my mind, I'll be Ya Ha Tinda bound
In my mind I'll be Ya Ha Tinda bound

by Scott Ward

Prologue

I saw the horses we were chasing enter the timber, followed moments later by Ron, Bert, and Donny, riding hard, pursued by a cloud of dust. My horse, Annabelle, and I were on the right course but were some distance behind. The mare reached out, stretching, covering as much ground as possible with each stride, as the wall of timber came closer and closer. Although the speed was exhilarating, a fleeting image of the mare tripping in a gopher hole crossed my mind. It was soon pushed aside by a rush of fear as we raced toward the seemingly impenetrable trees.

I had to slow things down; I needed to see if there were any snags or deadfall lurking in the shadows. No chance: we made the transition at full speed. For a second everything was black until my eyes had a chance to adjust to the changing light. Branches whipped by. The mare was caught in the thrill of the chase; all I could do was let her have her head and hope to stay in the saddle.

Annabelle dashed around a large spruce, then thundered toward some deadfall strung between two trees. It was going to hit me chest-high. With one hand on the reins and one hand clasping the saddle horn as an anchor, I braced myself for the collision. It exploded on impact — it was rotten and miraculously I was still in the saddle. It didn't take me long to realize that Annabelle had no game plan and was running just for the love of it.

Chapter 1
Backcountry Bound

he Millarville Mafia is the affectionate name given to a group of six individuals who were raised in Millarville, Alberta, during the late 1950s and early 1960s. This wild group of guys spent their early years chasing horses west of Millarville and doing a lot of youthful partying. They eventually settled down, however, and established successful careers in Canada's national parks. Five of the six worked for the outfitter Bert Mickle. Five of the six also went on to work for the warden service mainly in Banff National Park.

Bob Haney, CPW (Chief Park Warden) of several

national parks in the east, eventually became the CPW of Banff NP (National Park); Perry Jacobson, CPW of Kootenay NP, took over as the CPW of Banff NP when Bob retired; and Keith Foster became the CPW of Grassland NP in southern Saskatchewan. Donny Mickle, meanwhile, became the Cultural Resource Warden in Banff NP and spent many years as a park warden in Yoho NP, while John Nylund, for years a barn boss in Banff, became foreman of the government ranch (Ya Ha Tinda) west of Sundre, Alberta.

Dave Wildman was the only one not to pursue a career in the warden service, but he did work for Bert Mickle. He is now a successful rancher near Sangudo, Alberta, on the west bank of the Pembina River.

All the boys had strong ties to the land and their upbringing in the foothills of the Canadian Rockies — and saddlebags of stories to tell about life on the range.

* * *

It was early September, 1966, and a cold mist lay over the pony stand like a new fleece cloak as we rode out that morning for Temple Lodge. It had snowed briefly overnight, giving the landscape an airy feel. All I knew was that we were headed for the Skoki country and I was excited to be working in the mountains for the famous outfitter, Bert Mickle. The sun came out as we rode along the old Fish Creek Fire Road, headed for Temple Lodge and the trailhead. Our saddle horses were eager and prancing as we followed a small remuda of horses. Skip took the lead at the trailhead, while I fell in at the rear.

Only a day or so before, Skip Brochu had been hired by the Mickles for the fall hunting season. I got tossed into the mix because I was a friend of Skip's, and they needed two wranglers. For me, it was a rare opportunity to see some of Banff's more remote backcountry. I was just 20 and had no wilderness experience. Skip and I had chummed around that summer working as Brewster cowboys, taking dudes to the end of the lake and back. I had mastered the cowboy drawl and a walking swagger that was all-important for attracting the chambermaids and waitresses of Deer Lodge and the Chateau Lake Louise. Despite these distractions, we were still in need of a change. One-hour rides were kid's play compared to multi-day adventures with packhorses into unknown country. It was time to escape the endless partying and the repetitive daily rides.

Skip and I finally arrived at Temple Lodge late in the afternoon, where we were met unexpectedly by a slightly tipsy Bert Mickle. He was bridling a horse, while his wife, June, and two Millarville cowboys, Bob Haney and Keith Foster, looked on with concern. No one in the yard was impressed with Bert and his "Kid Shaleen" imitation parodying the 1965 western "Cat Ballou." Several of us still had to get to Skoki Lodge, and it was getting late. Skip and I corralled the horses and then walked up to the lodge where Keith and Bob were throwing supplies into a couple of sets of pack boxes. By now, Bert was sitting on the steps, a cigarette in his mouth, held in place by a tanned hand. He was supervising.

We walked over to Bert and he stood up stiffly, listing slightly to one side — he had a monstrously cranky back — and introduced himself. He already knew Skip. But I was a punk kid shaking hands with one of the toughest looking men you could imagine.

His appearance belied the fact that he had a heart of gold. He wore a stained and dusty Stetson that was originally black, but with all the trail grime on it, it could have been any colour. The curl on each side was flattened tight to the brim, giving him an eccentric but dangerous look. His long face was worn and weather-beaten and wrinkled, like the hide of an elephant. Big, black, bushy eyebrows shaded narrow eyes and his long sideburns came down level with his small, thin-lipped mouth. In the middle was a flattened nose, pasted to his face much like the brim of his hat. I gulped and said, "Hello," my voice squeaking.

Bert Mickle

Bert, his wife June, Skip and I, and a group of cowboys headed for Skoki that late afternoon with 20 loose horses. On the team were Bob Haney and Keith Foster. They were both from Millarville and were far more experienced with horses than I was. I watched them closely over the next few days, sizing them up; they paid little attention to me. Not to say they were unfriendly in any way, but they were about three or four years older than me, which is a big gap when you're only 20. Bob was the serious one and carried himself like he knew what he wanted out of life. Keith, who had worked for the outfit for the past several years, was lively and animated.

The first couple of kilometres of the trail wound through a forest of dark green spruce with patches of downy larch to an open sub-alpine meadow, which surrounded a hut — a small one-room cabin used by skiers in the winter on their way to Skoki Lodge. Built on a prominence overlooking the surrounding landscape, it was called Halfway Hut because it was located midway between the village of Lake Louise and Skoki. Bert called me "kid" as we rode on towards Boulder Pass and he pointed out the surrounding peaks: Redoubt, Ptarmigan, and Pika. Looking back, you could see the sweeping lines of the ski runs and the distant sentinels surrounding Lake Louise — Mounts Temple, Aberdeen, Lefroy, Victoria, and Whyte.

Soon we crested a bouldery crown of land, and there before us was Ptarmigan Lake, my first alpine lake. The trail skirted the shore to the left, then steadily angled up to a pass in the distance. As if on cue, everyone produced a bottle of whisky from his saddlebag. I accepted every offer to take a swig and felt my sobriety begin to wane.

The sight of horses and riders spread out ahead of me as we crossed the meadows heading for Deception Pass was exhilarating. At the summit of the pass, Bert Mickle charged around in high spirits, wielding a long pole like a lance — a western Don Quixote. Before long, Bert had fallen off his horse and everyone was howling with laughter. Bob Haney, disgusted with Bert's behaviour, headed off down into the Skoki Valley, leading the packhorses.

A short time later, I saw a column of smoke above the trees, and then the main lodge at Skoki came into view. Quite a group, including Bert and June's son, Donny, came out to meet us as we rode by to the corrals behind the lodge. It was a lively bunch that sat around the dinner table that night, telling stories and enjoying a few bottles of whisky.

Much later, I woke up in the dead of night in a strange bed. I had no idea were I was. Total darkness filled the room. I desperately needed to find a way out — my bladder was ready to burst. I groped around for the door and soon realized I was in a small room. I examined every crack and corner, until I finally brushed the latch. I stopped. My eyes were slowly adjusting to the scant moonlight and I could see a pitcher silhouetted next to a slowly materializing window. With relief, I peed into it, then found the bed and went back to sleep.

Next morning, I heard a knock and was up in a flash. I called out that I'd be right down, grabbed the pitcher, and dumped the contents out the window. I had the pitcher in my hand as I went downstairs, intending to rinse it in the creek before going to breakfast, but Bert surprised me at the bottom of the stairs as I snuck toward the door. I stashed the pitcher next to a small bookshelf. I didn't want Bert to know that I had used his lovely enamel pitcher with its unique floral design as a urinal. He asked me to bring in some wood for the fire.

When I got back inside, everyone greeted me with questions about how I felt, how my head felt —with barely concealed chuckles. Bob looked at me as though I was a neophyte that had just gone through an initiation. "Get used to it if you're going to work for this outfit!" he said with a laugh. I had drunk too much the night before and it was all coming back to me now.

Bert asked me to go down to the corral and let Keith and Donny know breakfast was ready. Off I went again and when I got back, I searched madly for the pitcher, but it was nowhere to be found. Quietly, I slipped into the dining room and sat down for breakfast with everyone else. I reached for a slice of toast and then watched in frozen horror as Bert poured himself some juice from a very familiar pitcher. He brought the glass to his thin lips and drank. An expression passed over his face, a delicate hesitation or reflection, more quizzical than anything else — as though he was trying to identify something, an aftertaste, subtle but distinct. Then, as suddenly as the expression was there, it was gone, and he poured himself another glass. If I admitted to my secret it would be the shortest job I ever had.

Skip headed back to Temple that day, while a small group of us were assigned to trailing the horses out to the Siffleur Wilderness for the start of hunting season. Bob and Keith took up the lead; Donny Mickle and I followed, driving the horses down the trail to the Little Pipestone. Shortly after leaving Skoki, we skirted Merlin Meadows on our descent to the Pipestone River. Donny pointed out Merlin's Castle as we passed, a rock formation up to the left above the cirque that held the lake of the same name. In two hours, we arrived at the Little Pipestone warden cabin and forded the Pipestone River.

It is a pleasant ride up the Pipestone from this point. The trail passes through old stands of jack pine, dissected here and there by meadows, as it wanders close to the river. When we eventually broke out of the trees onto a small height of land, there, spread out before us, lay Singing Meadows. A meandering stream ran through the meadow, clear and blue. Off to the right, across the valley, Singing Falls slipped down a smooth rock face adding a magical touch to the place. We felt compelled to stop and drink in the surroundings.

Nearing Pipestone Pass, we came upon an old warden cabin and stopped for lunch. The cabin had scratches all over its logs; some were deeply furrowed, while others seemed fresher. I asked Keith how they had gotten there and he told me grizzly bears had raked their claws over it trying to get in.

After lunch we continued up to Pipestone Pass. The notch of the pass marked our descent into the Siffleur Valley. The undulating terrain of the upper Siffleur, with its carpet of soft vegetation sprinkled with small patches of alpine fir and full of hidden pockets and depressions, is ideal for concealing the caribou that are known to live here. Sightings, however, are rare. We found their tracks, but the caribou eluded us. Today, if you are lucky and take the time to look around, you might catch sight of some caribou cooling off away from the flies in the shade of an east-facing snow field, where they're easier to spot.

Krumholtz (small clumps of alpine fir) started to appear around us as we headed down the Siffleur Valley and we soon came to a trail junction. To our right was Clearwater Pass, its summit rolling back 170 metres above us. We continued down valley and eventually broke out into an old burn area. Scattered about were young pine trees growing up around the charred deadfall. This was to be our campsite for the night and it offered us a view of Dolomite Valley and the Siffleur Wilderness.

The campsite was called Wildman Camp. It provided only the basics: running water, firewood, and a view. We unloaded the two packhorses and turned them out. It didn't take long to prepare supper, requiring only a can opener and some heat, and we settled in. With great glee, Donny reached into one of the pack boxes and pulled out a bottle of whisky, which he swiftly uncorked — in hindsight, much too easily. He tossed the bottle back and took a swig, then spit it out. Without warning, he began to curse his sister, Faye: she had replaced the contents of the bottle with tea! What Keith called her was not flattering. I was to find out later that there was no match for Keith Foster's mouth in a situation like this. Bob mumbled something about all the Mickles being the same and retired for the night.

Breakfast brought forth yet more scorn. We were off early with hollow stomachs as our eggs were only shells that morning. Faye had blown the contents out through holes at each end. Her name came up frequently over the next hour or two and not in any pleasant way.

Later that morning we arrived at the Dolomite

stream crossing, a wide and boulder-strewn one at that, and it took us awhile to coax the horses across. But before too long we were in a deep, mossy forest that offered little in the way of scenery. Finally we crossed the park boundary — a narrow slash up through the trees, perpendicular to the trail. The path we were following meandered through the timber for another three kilometres before breaking out into a small clearing. From here you could see the start of a seismic road. It was near here that Bert maintained his hunting camp. The eventful trip was almost over.

As the four of us sat around the fire that night, little did we know that we would all follow the same course and join the warden service. Bob would soon be working in Waterton Lakes National Park as a seasonal park warden, while Keith would do the same in Jasper. Donny's career in the warden service would start in Yoho and mine here in Lake Louise.

Chapter 2
Spring Round-Up

My life as a cowboy started when I was 20 years old when I went to work for the Mickle family, outfitters from the Millarville area just southwest of Calgary. My real initiation, however, took place six months later. The spring round-up on the Red Deer River not far from the Ya Ha Tinda government horse ranch was two weeks of hard riding over a lot of rough country.

The first task for the cowboys involved in the round-up was to catch all the horses that had been wintered on the open range, then trail them up to Scotch Camp just inside Banff National Park. There, we would ride some of them down to take the spring buck out of them. The round-up culminated in a 60 km ride up the Red Deer River to Red Deer Lakes and then over into the Pipestone Valley and down to Lake Louise.

The first morning, and every morning of the round-up, we saddled up and crossed the Red Deer River. It was swollen from spring run-off and the horses were forced to swim. It was a cold wake-up call, as we got soaked to our waists sitting on our horses. Once on the far shore, we followed a seismic line perpendicular to the river up a steep hill until we reached the head of a large meadow that stretched south for several kilometres. The four of us — Bert Mickle, Donny Mickle, Ron Hall, and myself — rode into this expanse with our eyes peeled, looking for signs of horses. I was on a dark, bay mare called Annabelle. She was fast, but I knew little else about her.

We soon spotted a herd of horses grazing in the middle of the meadow some distance off. As we moved up on them, they spotted us and started running towards the timber's edge a kilometre away. We broke out in a lope, heading after them. Annabelle took off with the rest of the group, but instead of heading in the right direction, she ran at a 30-degree angle away from the others, stretching out, happy just to run. I tried to turn her, but she was too headstrong to pull around. Finally, I had to rein her in to a complete stop, turn her in the right direction, and then kick her into a gallop. The rest of the group was now well ahead of us, but we at least had something to pursue.

I saw the group of horses enter the timber followed closely by Ron, Bert, and Donny. Annabelle and I were on the right course but still some distance behind. After entering the trees at full speed, and narrowly avoiding being knocked out of the saddle by rotten deadfall, I realized that Annabelle had no game plan and was running just for the love of it. By now we had completely lost contact with the others. I brought her to a stop after a sustained effort. I had lost confidence in this horse's ability to follow the chase.

We rode back across the meadow, northward, towards camp in an antsy trot; she wanted to run, and I had to work at keeping her reined in. Eventually, we settled into a brisk walk back to the river's edge. I felt like a dismal failure as we swam back across the river. I wondered how the rest were making out.

Back at camp, June Mickle was no help. "Dale, after all that riding, where are the horses?"

"Well, June," I answered wearily, "if I knew, I wouldn't be here now." I glumly cast my eyes towards the fire. Sensing she had touched a nerve, she asked me if I wanted some coffee.

It seemed like a very long time, but was probably

no more than a few hours, when I heard horses splashing in the river. The group had returned and had been successful in capturing about 15 head — a good start to the round-up. Everyone settled around the fire with a cup of coffee and went over how the events of the day had unfolded. They laughed as each took turns telling his story of the chase. I stoked the fire and made sure there was fresh coffee, listening to the stories with envy.

My saddle horse the next day was White Ranger, a leggy, grey thoroughbred with a hard mouth who had lots of speed, but, as I soon found out, little else. Each of us rode off in a different direction to find the horses. Our theory was, once one of us located them, we would report back and put a plan in place to round the horses up.

White Ranger and I were working our way up a hill in the timber, when he suddenly stopped. Standing quietly in the trees in front of us was a small herd of horses looking like they had been caught in a game of hide-and-seek. Many had the shaggy, thick appearance of a wild horse, but several had the slicker coats of groomed, ranch-bred horses. They started to move off to the right, then suddenly took off. Generally, the strategy was to try and stick with them until they tired and then attempt to herd them in the right direction, but this required the help of a second rider. I knew I was supposed to report back with their location, but that plan lost its appeal as the excitement of a chase grew in my mind. Although the likelihood of being successful by myself was remote, I decided to stick with them and see what happened.

White Ranger and I burst into a meadow at the top of the hill, only to see the tail end of the herd ahead of us. For some reason, I thought I could rope one of them. But as I looked down for the lariat, I was suddenly swept out of the saddle by a large, overhanging branch. I landed on my backside and saw White Ranger racing off ahead. I got up and ran after him as fast as I could, yelling for him to stop, but my riding boots and shotgun chaps slowed me down. Fortunately, the bridle rains were dragging beside him, slowing him down. I continued to yell until I finally managed to get up to him and grab the reins. I couldn't believe my luck and, within seconds, I was back on him and we were streaking over the crest of the hill trying to catch up to the rest of the horses.

I'd never been on a horse that ran so fast. I was riding pretty loose, just trying to stay with him as trees flashed by. We raced madly over the top of a flat, open summit, and then a gully suddenly appeared on the right. White Ranger veered wildly to the left, almost pitching me out of the saddle and onto the ground again. Somehow, I managed to hook the toe of my riding boot on the cantle of the saddle and claw myself back

into the seat. I grabbed on to everything within reach —
saddle strings, slickers, even bags.

We hit the trees again and eventually caught up to
the horses as they rocketed downhill through a stand of
poplar. We were bouncing off trees like balls in a pinball
machine. Soon, rails started to appear on my right, then
on my left, and I couldn't believe my luck. These were
the long wings of a catch corral, set in place specifically
to capture wild horses. I could see the horses bunching
up ahead of me as the corral reached out to contain
them.

They were now all in the corral, and I thought,
"Wow! Bert is going to be proud of me when I show him
all the horses I caught single-handed on my first big
chase." But the show wasn't over yet. I needed to dis-
mount quickly to slide the rails across the front of the
corral to hold the herd, but my horse wouldn't stop. I
pulled on the reins as hard as I could, but Ranger had
the bit in his mouth and we plunged forward until we hit
the fence at the back of the corral. I looked over my
shoulder only to see the horses dashing out of the corral
and up the hill. We stood there, the two of us, Ranger's
sides heaving and me gaping in hatless amazement,
while his tongue worked the bit in his frothy mouth. It
was over. They had got away and I started to feel the
pain in my knees from the poplar trees we had hit on the

way down. Later, we rode up to the top of the hill and started down the other side. I found the spot where I had been knocked off by the branch, marked by my missing cowboy hat.

I met up with the rest of the group later and told my tale of missed opportunity. A few hours later, we ran into the same bunch of horses and were off crashing through the timber again. For Ranger and I, however, the chase was over. He was spent from the morning chase and soon we lost contact with the group, but not before I lost my hat again. I spent some time searching for it, but never found it. I got a good ribbing from everyone later. We eventually herded the horses into camp and spent the remainder of the day making repairs around the camp. Bert gave me a blue polka-dot cap as a memento of my missed opportunity and I often wore it over the next few years when I chased horses.

A few days later, a couple of friends of the Mickles' showed up — Dave Wildman and Ivor Lister. They were two Millarville cowboys with lots of horse chasing experience. Dave had worked for Bert a few years earlier. Ivor was the brother of Jerry Lister, a park warden at Red Deer Lakes. The next day, because of the added manpower, Bert decided we would ride down to The Corners forestry cabin and try to round up as many horses as possible on the way through. June decided to join us on

From left to right: the author, Bert Mickle, Donny Mickle,
and Laurie McChonachy

the ride, and with her red hat and buckskin jacket, she
added colour to the group. I was still hoping to be of
some use on this round-up and I had a gut feeling that
today would be the day.

Again we found ourselves riding south through the
first big meadow, until we entered the timber at its
southern end. Two of the group rode off to the left to
check out a hidden meadow, while the rest of us continued to ride south through the trees. Before too long, we

flushed a few horses out of the bush. Not wanting to push them too hard, we fell in behind them at a gentle trot. Soon they were joined by other horses that seemed to just appear. Almost by accident, we had a small band trotting ahead of us.

We broke into another open meadow, the horses growing in number. No sooner had we emerged into the open than their leader put his head down, bucked a few times, and took off. That was the signal for the rest to follow as they madly galloped south. We were picking up horses everywhere. Suddenly, there was a crashing noise to our left and out of the timber came about 20 head of horses and a few bewildered elk followed by a couple of yelling cowboys. Eighty horses now spread out before us in a wave of undulating colour as we galloped at full speed toward The Corners. Excitement mounted as we swept forward, followed by a cloud of dust and exhilarating shouts from the trailing riders.

On each side, a rider moved up steadily on the outside, trying to contain the stretched-out herd and prevent any from breaking off, directing them all the while towards The Corners. It wasn't necessary, though, as the horses seemed to know the routine and the chase was all that counted now. Mud and gravel flew past our heads off the hooves of the horses in front as we raced over the country. Our faces spattered with mud, we were none-the-less thrilled with the spectacle of racing animals. All that remained was to corral them at the end of the chase. After eight kilometres of hard riding, we saw The Corners. As if on signal, the horses slowed down enough for us to guide them easily into the big corral.

We had captured more than just Mickle horses. We spent some time sorting the herd out and releasing some of the other horses. After a rare opportunity for a lunch break, seldom enjoyed on the trail back then, we began the task of trailing the horses back to our camp on the Red Deer River. Ron and I went up front to lead the procession, while the rest followed up, urging the horses along as needed. We had to set a good pace that would keep the horses moving without bunching them up. Allowing them to feel crowded could set them running past us. The riders in the rear had to be careful not to push the horses too aggressively. It was all a matter of subtle judgment, and after a few kilometres, the horses start to string out in single file and settle into an easy pace. A pecking order was established that the horses would adhere to for the remainder of the day.

After 10 days of hard, exhilarating pursuit, we successfully rounded up all the horses and shod a good many of them. We were now set to trail them through to Lake Louise.

The next morning saw us leave the Big Horn

Campsite with a hundred head of horses, followed by June Mickle driving the truck with the camp on board. Things stayed relatively tame as we negotiated the winding road leading across the Ya Ha Tinda between our former campsite and the distant mountains we were headed to. Then everything changed as we entered open country.

Once the horses hit the flat, they burst into a gallop. A few threw their heads down, kicking and bucking, and started to charge past Bert who was in the lead. I could hear him yelling as he rode hard to keep ahead. The whole herd was now in pursuit, fanning out as we tried to keep them flanked. After a couple of kilometres, they finally settled into a nice easy lope along the fire road leading to Scotch Camp, our destination that first day out.

Thing progressed well until we neared West Lakes, the western boundary of the ranch. The night before, Bert and Donny had predicted that White Lady and her bunch would make a break from the main group, and they did. They were now headed north towards the lakes, the rest of the horses following Bert westward. I stayed with the main group, while Donny and Ron rode out to cut White Lady's group off. Soon the main group started to swing north, too, and I rode hard to keep them flanked; Bert kept heading west with a few loyal supporters. Eventually, Donny and Ron outflanked White Lady's group and bent them westward towards the main herd. Bert picked up his speed and broke into a gallop. With a lot of yelling, I chased the horses back onto the road behind Bert where, once again, they strung out on the trail to Scotch Camp.

Scotch Camp is the staging area for two back-country warden districts and has a large pasture, well fenced with a good set of corrals. It's strategically located just off a fire road that, back then, led to Banff town site, 48 kilometres away. It's an attractive log structure with separate sleeping quarters from the dining room and kitchen area. Jimmy Simpson — the son of Jimmy Simpson Sr., a legend in the Canadian Rockies — and his wrangler, Jeff Wilson, greeted us when we arrived. Both based out of Num-Ti-Jah Lodge in Banff National Park, they were also there to round up horses.

Simpson and Wilson's horses wintered up near the Tyrell Creek Flats, which sits on the north side of the Red Deer River and just west of the park boundary. Jeff Wilson was Jimmy's packer and spent the summer months working out of the pony stand at Num-Ti-Jah Lodge. When hunting season arrived, he would turn his attention to cooking on those fall trips.

That afternoon, Bert rounded up the colts and fillies and some older horses that needed to be "topped off" every spring. We all gathered down at the corrals to watch Ron Hall ride the buck out of one of the colts. This was a great way to end the day after an invigorating ride from the government ranch, and I was enjoying every minute of it. It was exciting to watch someone else riding a green-broke colt from behind the safety of the fence.

Donny was the next one up. Bert passed around a bottle of whisky and each of us took a pull from it. I was enjoying a good swig when my perfect day fell apart. Donny was trotting a now submissive three-year-old around the corral, waving at us like we were spectators at the Stampede Parade. Bert leaned over the fence, looked at me, and said, "All right kid, you're next." A knot of fear formed in my throat. I thought this show was for experienced hands only; I was just a spectator. But there was no escaping Bert.

The first horse I climbed on bucked me off, leaving me dusting myself off and chasing him unceremoniously around the corral. I climbed back on and rode him until he quit bucking, which seemed to take forever.

My shirt was now hanging outside my blue jeans as I rode the second colt. As the horse kicked skyward, I felt a tug on my shirt, and most of the buttons popped off like a zipper. I was bounced around all over that saddle, as the colt worked out his pent-up energy. On one or two occasions I came down well forward of the saddle and I considered myself fortunate that I didn't land smack on the saddle-horn. Magically, I stayed on him; I even earned a round of cheers from my whisky-drinking audience. I rode a couple more and by the end of the day I was pretty sore from the pounding I had taken in the saddle and from the rough bounces on the ground.

Thinking back, the day's events are a blur of adrenaline, excitement, and whisky. I suppose I passed some sort of initiation test that day, but at the time, that was the farthest thing from my mind. More importantly, I had survived. I received pats on the back for making it an entertaining afternoon — it certainly had been, for everyone but me.

A lively night followed. Everyone sat around the table swapping stories as bottles of rum and whisky appeared from various duffels. Bert and Jimmy were old friends, and Jeff knew everyone there, except me. I sat back and watched it all, and after such an eventful day, I was the first to hit the hay. I woke up early, about five in the morning, to feed and water the horses in the corral. Jimmy Simpson, Jeff Wilson, and Bert Mickle's brother-in-law, Norm Smith, were still up, sitting around the table with a nearly-spent bottle of Hudson Bay over-proof rum. It was parked in the middle of the table, attracting them like moths to a light.

In those days, the relationship between outfitters

and park wardens was a lot closer than it is today. There was very little backpacking activity in the more remote areas of the park, outside of the odd mountaineering party attempting to bag a faraway peak. The outfitters, who spent their summer in the park, were a reliable source of information for the district warden. They became an extra set of eyes and ears. This mutual association also provided a natural stepping stone for anyone who wanted to start a career in the warden service.

Having taken care of the horses, I came back to the cabin and rousted everyone out of bed. The rest of the horses could be seen out in the middle of the meadow. After breakfast, we rounded them up and headed out. We trailed the horses through to Lake Louise, a distance of 60 kilometres. It was the start of another great summer in the mountains.

Chapter 3
Annabelle Goes AWOL

Donny and Faye were the son and daughter of Bert and June Mickle, a family of pioneering stock. Bert was a horseman, guide, and trapper; June was an artist with a good business sense. The Mickle clan was from the foothills country west of Millarville, some of the most captivating cattle country in western Canada. They were looking to exchange that for the scenery around Lake Louise and a new life in some of the most majestic mountain landscapes in the world.

Back in the summer of 1962, the Mickles were in the process of buying Timberline Tours from the colourful Lake Louise outfitter, Ray Lagace. The family was going to spend the year learning the country, the horses, and the business operation from the old mountain man. Not only were they buying an outfitting business but also the lease to a couple of lodges owned by Sir Norman Watson. Sir Norman was from Britain and the owner of the Lake Louise ski area. One lease included the famous back-country lodge at Skoki and the other included Temple Lodge. Temple was at the end of the road on the back side of the Lake Louise ski area, conveniently situated at the trailhead for the Red Deer Lakes and Skoki country.

Donny was a blond, wavy-haired youth of 19 with a tall, lean look, who fit confidently into his surroundings. His sister Faye, a couple of years younger, had darker features, more characteristic of her father. It was hard to believe, though, after meeting Bert, that he had had anything to do with her beauty. Decked out in their soft, homemade leather clothing, the siblings were a stunning pair.

Donny worked that summer at Skoki Lodge, learning what he could of the country from old Ray. He cut wood and hauled water for the cooks; he jingled horses in the early hours of the morning; he helped guide the clients that used Skoki as a base for their trips; and he travelled the country.

One of Donny's jobs was to pack customers into Skoki on horseback and take them on day trips out of that venerable lodge using the small herd kept there for that purpose. Every morning, he would round up the horses that had been turned out the night before. It was not practical to keep a large amount of hay at the lodge so each night bells were fixed to the horses and they were let loose to forage for themselves.

Bert and June spent their time at the pony stand, which is still located behind Deer Lodge at Lake Louise. They concentrated on the business and the booking end of the operation, as well as leading the one- and two-hour rides that departed from there. Faye divided her attention between Skoki, the pony stand, and the family farm near Millarville.

Ray had between 80 and 100 head of horses that were scattered between Skoki, the pony stand in Lake Louise, Temple, and Point Camp — 18 kilometres up the Pipestone River from Lake Louise. Point Camp was where Ray kept the horses that were not being used, those horses that were infirm or simply in need of a rest from the trail. It consisted of a small tent camp with a corral located next to a huge meadow. Here, the horses roamed freely in the open grassland.

One morning, at first light, Donny, along with fellow wrangler, Richard Regnier, went down to the corral to get their saddle horses. Three horses had been kept in that night, one of which was Donny's saddle horse, Annabelle.

Annabelle loved to run. Not for any particular purpose, but just for the pure pleasure of running. She was a leggy, dark bay mare of medium build. She had a narrow, irregular white blaze on her handsome face that accentuated a finely featured head. Annabelle was also an unusually intelligent horse and would have made a fine saddle horse, if she could only have given up her wild urge to run. That said, she was still a good mount for a rider with a firm hand.

The two blurry-eyed wranglers saddled their horses in silence. Quickly they mounted and rode off. They shivered in the cool morning air as they hunkered down and headed towards Merlin Meadows, a kilometre below Skoki. Little was said until they broke out into the meadow. There was no sign of the horses, but there were fresh tracks heading farther down the valley. Donny quickly realized the worst had happened — the horses had managed to break through the drift fence during the night and were headed down the valley. Another three kilometres along the trail was a meadow, where Donny hoped the horses might have stopped to feed before pursuing their quest for freedom. Sure enough, in the middle of the meadow stood the delinquent horses. As Donny remarked later about Annabelle, "She was a nice horse, but as soon as she got whiff of chasing something, she was totally uncontrollable."

As if by signal, the horses stopped feeding and looked up at the two forlorn riders. Richard and Donny approached cautiously, trying to circle around to the left of them. They wanted to station themselves between the horses and the direction they were headed. It didn't work. The horses bolted and the chase was on. Richard and Donny madly tried to cut them off, but the horses had too much of a lead. They were quickly into the trees and running hard. As Donny followed into the woods, he saw a low branch directly in his path. He tried to pull Annabelle up, but there was slim hope of that. She had already picked out her route and it was directly under the branch. She drove Donny straight into the bony limb and it swept him out of the saddle and onto his backside. Donny remembers being kind of knocked out and getting a big bump on his head. The last he saw of Annabelle was her rump undulating in pursuit of the rapidly disappearing horses. She never looked back. Donny got up and brushed himself off. There was nothing to do but start walking back to Skoki.

He hobbled into Skoki Lodge, and there was Ray with all the guests, sitting in the kitchen. Now, old Ray was famous for his lisp. When he saw Donny, he exclaimed, "Jethus Donny. What did you do? You've lotht your horthe and thaddle and you look like hell! Now, I think you're going to be riding thkin ath [skin ass or bareback] for a while." He added, "You better take old Midnight, the only horthe left in the corral. Yeth, you've done very well, Mithter Mickle."

Donny got little sympathy and a few hours later, Richard returned with most of the horses; but there was no Annabelle. Richard had last seen her running crazy through the bush, past all the horses, headed in the direction of the Pipestone Valley. Donny climbed on Midnight — bareback — and headed in the direction the horses were last seen with little in the way of food and no concrete game plan. He'd had enough of Ray's sarcastic wit and he was concerned for Annabelle's well-being.

For two days, Donny rode with little rest and only a quick meal as he occasionally passed by Skoki. He covered all the surrounding countryside, all the meadows and favourite horse haunts with no luck. Then on the third day, he found himself down in the Pipestone. In a meadow just east of where the trail from Skoki reaches the Pipestone Valley, he found a piece of rein from his bridle. Annabelle had been here for a while at least. He headed for Point Camp, six kilometres downstream to see if she had been drawn there by the presence of the other horses.

At Point Camp, by chance Donny met his dad who had heard of the missing horse by "moccasin telegraph." Bert had come up to look for Annabelle as well. Donny was relieved to see Bert — he was someone who had chased many a wild horse in his younger days, quite a bushman and a good tracker. Soon they had parcelled up the country they would each search. Neither had any food with them, so they spent time trying to catch a few bull-trout in the river.

With no fishing rods or line, they tried to stun the fish by throwing rocks at them, and this worked in a limited fashion. In time, they had a couple of fish. They found an old enamel plate, built a fire, and cooked the fish. That was their lunch. They then separated and Bert headed up the Pipestone, while Donny headed for the Red Deer Lakes country adjacent to the Skoki area. That was the last they would see of each other for quite a while.

Donny returned to Skoki that night, where he expected to meet Bert before heading off to Red Deer Lakes the next morning. When Bert didn't show up, Donny left early the next day on his own, bareback again on old Midnight. After checking out the meadows around the lakes, he headed downstream 12 kilometres towards Horseshoe Lakes. At the Sandhills warden cabin, he met district warden Jerry (Red) Lister. Red eyed Donny up and down.

"Why are you bareback on that old packhorse?" he asked with a frown on his face.

"I've ridden four days, looking for my horse and my gear," Donny answered, filling him in on the details.

"Well there's no horse sign around here," Red said. He tied off the diamond on top of his packhorse and then swung up into his saddle and rode off with a grin on his face. "I guess riding bareback ain't all that bad. But if I spot your horse or saddle, I'll send a message out to your dad."

In the meantime, when Bert and Donny parted company Bert headed up the Pipestone Valley to check out a long string of open meadows beside the river. A couple of kilometres past the warden cabin, where the Little Pipestone enters the Pipestone River, he found a fresh horse track on the trail. Bert was riding an old horse called Chico. Chico was like a bloodhound and had a reputation for tracking horses. He was a popular horse to keep in at night and ride in the morning when you went looking for your "cayuses." He would sniff the ground then take off in a trot, and you just hung on until he found them. Many a horse, turned out for the night, has looked up in disgust the next morning on seeing old Chico approach.

When Bert found the track, old Chico bent down

and sniffed the black earth. His nostrils flared fully and he snorted hard, like a bellows on a flame. He lifted his head and looked up the valley. Without further ado, he headed out in a slow easy trot: it was 18 kilometres to Pipestone Pass. Bert kept his eye to the ground. The fresh horse droppings were encouraging. It didn't look like the horse they were following had ever stopped to eat.

When Chico and Bert reached Singing Meadows they stopped to look around. There was no sign of Annabelle, so they kept riding. Chico never hesitated — he had a job to do and a track to follow. The horse travelled at a steady trot and Bert was impressed with Chico's new-found energy. The countryside went by with considerable ease.

They reached the old Upper Pipestone warden cabin marked with grizzly claw scrapes on its logs, but still no sign of Annabelle. Then finally, they broke out of the trees four kilometres from Pipestone Pass. For a moment, Bert thought he saw the silhouette of a horse on the skyline of the pass, but he wasn't sure. Even up hill, Chico's pace didn't slacken, until finally they crested the summit, and there was Annabelle, looking wild and crazy. She stood there, trembling in terror as if the first misstep would send her off on another panicky run. There wasn't much left of the saddle on her back. It was perched precariously in place, held by the rear cinch that had slipped back, and was now flanking her. It was barely a saddle as the stirrups, front cinch, breast collar, and bridle had been stripped off by her close encounters with the trees.

Bert approached on Chico, ever aware that Annabelle could bolt at any moment. The horse was crazy with fear as they drew close, and Annabelle swung with lightning speed, kicking Chico in the chest. Chico didn't even flinch, and again they approached. Suddenly, Annabelle bolted, forcing Chico and Bert to follow in pursuit. As she ran across the pass, Chico came up behind her. Annabelle cocked her leg and fired again, kicking Chico in the shoulder, narrowly missing Bert's leg. Bert swung Chico around and managed to cut Annabelle off. She came to an abrupt halt. Ever so carefully and with a soothing voice, he dismounted. He spoke to her for a long time with that same soft voice and eventually managed to get within arm's reach.

He started by slowly touching her chest and trembling shoulder as he talked to her. Concealed behind his back in his other hand, he held several loops of a rope. Annabelle was coiled like a spring, quivering, but she stayed where she was. She seemed to understand that all this was necessary. Slowly, he worked his hand up her neck until he was standing next to her. In a comforting tone, he whispered placating noises as he carefully moved his hand over her nose. At this point, she relented and buried her head into his armpit, releasing all the tension from her body. After he placed the rope around her neck and improvised a halter, he went about trying to take the saddle off. While all this was going on, Chico fed quietly on some nearby plants as if nothing had happened. The saddle readjusted and secured in place, Bert mounted Chico and took off for Lake Louise leading Annabelle. Chico was stepping out like a colt again, satisfied everything had turned out well.

The next day a pack string arrived from Temple, and Donny found out, to his great relief, that Annabelle had been found. Meanwhile Ray's pack trip was nearly over, so Donny rushed off to meet up with the group. When he caught up to them later that day, "moccasin telegraph" had already reached them.

"Yeth Donny, you're pretty good with people, and you can shoe a horthe well, but your father's a much better horthe-turd detective than you are," Ray said to Donny as he rode into camp.

Chapter 4
Donny and Keith's Horse Trip

eith Foster had a great aversion to the taste of beans. He had no fondness for them as a kid in Millarville, but when he went to work for Bert Mickle in Lake Louise, he grew to hate them. Donny Mickle tolerated them more than Keith, but then he would eat almost anything. If he was hungry, he just opened the fridge and grabbed whatever was closest on the shelf. Although Donny thought ketchup could turn anything into *haute cuisine*, even beans took their toll after a while.

The Mickles seemed to have an abundance of beans and they showed up without fail in the pack boxes on every horse trip. We would complain like a broken record to Bert and June, but those beans would always turn up among the other canned goods that were so popular in the can-happy 1960s. Beans extended a pot of stew for up to a week on the trail. After the second day, Bert would add a few cans of beans to the pot for each additional night. This increased the volume, but also diluted the concentration of meat and vegetables. To give the stew some colour and zip, he often added a can or two of Mexican-style corn. My abiding memory of Bert is of him leaning over a fire, stirring another can of something into the pot, a cigarette dangling from his lips, its long ash hanging precariously from the end. Inevitably, this, too, would be added to the stew.

The year before I started to work for the Mickle outfit, Donny and Keith made a long trip from their hunting area in the Blackstone, north of Nordegg, Alberta, to the country just south of the Ya Ha Tinda Ranch on the Red Deer River. They had been assigned the chore of trailing the horses back to their wintering grounds. The two wranglers were looking forward to the trip, as they would be riding through country they hadn't seen in a while.

Now, Keith resembled a cartoon caricature; he had no chin and one eye that often drooled. A silk neckerchief, which he wore proudly around his skinny neck, added colour to this simple picture. The neckerchief, as well as the rest of his western attire, would eventually become a signature of his style.

It was late October, and the region was enjoying one of those cherished spells of Indian summer. The days were blessed with deep blue skies, while warm winds caressed the land in the evenings. This is often the best time to be out on a trip in the montane grasslands of the Frontal Range. You know winter is just around the corner, and the threat of snow makes the season all the more special.

Donny's sister, Faye, and the last of the season's clients joined the cowboys on the long haul to the road. It was Faye's job to then repack the boxes for Donny and Keith's trip back to the wintering ground south of the Ya Ha Tinda.

Like lazy slugs used to a routine, Donny and Keith lingered around the fire while Faye packed up provisions for them. They ignored her complaints that this was an unjust world; she wondered why she couldn't be trailing the horses instead of Keith or Donny. Keith only inflamed the situation by offering his opinions on the role of women and suggesting that Faye should shut up and accept it. To say that Keith could be boorish and obtuse towards Donny's sister was an understatement. Keith would rue that moment later and wonder why he hadn't anticipated her revenge.

They were off early the next morning and were surprised when Faye handed them a lunch each. This was an unusual gesture on Faye's part and it baffled Donny. Keith accepted it with no further thought. It would be their only meal on the long 45-km ride that first day. Donny took the lead, leaving Keith to bring up the rear, as they headed west for the Kootenay Plains. They were in good spirits as they rode along the gravel road. Between the riders were 18 head of horses including two packhorses carrying their food and camp gear. Keith was always hungry and he wondered what treat might be in store for him at supper that night. He hoped for some left over meatloaf from the previous night's dinner. He loved meatloaf and, what's more, they wouldn't even need to heat it up. With that thought in mind, he pulled out his lunch. He looked at the skimpy sandwich. All seemed right; he saw some mustard announcing the presence of some meat, at least, and so, with great anticipation, he bit into it.

"God damn it, Mickle!" Keith bellowed. "That miserable woman. I'm going to kill your sister!" With that, Donny was brought up to date on the state of Keith's sandwich. Faye had diligently laid between two pieces of stale bread two slices of waxed paper, much as you would processed cheese. Spread over the paper was a skimpy amount of mustard. In one corner lay the imprint of Keith's false teeth. Disgusted, he tossed the sandwich into the bush.

Donny escaped with marginally better sandwiches: two slices of bread with mustard, ketchup, and nothing else. But to Donny, this was no hardship.

It wasn't until they approached the Kootenay Plains, where they would camp for the first night, that Keith indicated he was in better spirits. They camped down by the river in a grove of aspen, with an unobstructed view of the mountains to the west. It had been a hot summer and there was not even a hint of white on the distant mountains.

Keith was hungry and before long he dived into the pack boxes, removing layers of jackets and pants until he finally reached the food at the bottom of the boxes. All he found were tins of beans. Two rows of goddamn beans. He let out a scream that got Donny's immediate and alarmed attention. Donny started into the second set of boxes only to find pots and pans and kitchen utensils, but no food. Keith's eyes darted around the scattered camp. He began kicking things and cursing Faye. All Donny could do was watch. As close as he and Faye were, there was no love lost between them at moments like this.

They had enough beans to last at least a week or so,

but that was small comfort when the only accompaniment was a half loaf of bread and a jar of sandwich spread. Simmering with resentment, they unrolled their bedrolls on the ground and threw the tent over them like a quilt. They built a fire and made sandwiches using the sandwich spread. Not the most appetizing meal, but better than canned beans.

The sound of horse bells awoke them the next morning. It was a promising morning. Donny got up first and lit a small fire. Neither spoke a word as they dressed, grabbed their halters, and set off to retrieve the horses. It was comforting to find them nearby. After a breakfast of cold beans on the little bread that was left, they were off for the White Rabbit Valley.

Keith knew the country well and stationed himself in the lead; Donny took up the rear, pushing the stragglers along. For the whole day, they saw little of each other as the horses spaced themselves out and settled into a reasonable pecking order. The wranglers had no lunch and after a barely palatable breakfast, they anticipated their arrival at the Indianhead warden station. Here, they hoped to run into the resident warden and a welcoming evening meal. First though, they had to ascend the pass at the head of the White Rabbit River and climb the upper reaches of the Ram River. From there it was over another pass to Indianhead

Donny and Keith's Horse Trip

Creek and Banff National Park.

Indianhead warden station is rather an unusual place. It sits in an open field of poplar and spruce, surrounded by a white pole fence, miles from any road. A bungalow in the middle of the wilderness strikes the unwary traveller as odd, yet intriguing and welcoming at the same time. Donny and Keith had been there before and they had always been greeted by friendly and hospitable wardens. They envisioned the same this day, being invited to stay for the night and fed a hearty meal.

It was dusk when the pair pushed their 18 head of horses into the pasture near the station. They could see the warden's horses jumping around a small corral with their bells and hobbles on. They were met on the doorstep of the cabin by Jim Rimmer. Jim was an eccentric Englishman who had recently joined the warden service and already had a reputation as someone less than hospitable. The fact that it was almost dark didn't add to his disposition.

He talked to Donny and Keith for a few minutes, asking questions as though he were interrogating them. Who were they, where were they going, and what were they up to? They told him that they worked for Bert Mickle, and they were heading for their winter range on the Red Deer River with 18 head of horses. Jim took all of this in and replied in his English accent, "Well you boys look a little hungry, perhaps I can rustle you up a spud." On hearing what sounded like a novel term for supper, they went in and sat down at the table keeping up a lively conversation about the fortuitous Indian summer they were having.

Meanwhile, Jim took a potato, a fairly small one, and cut it into little slices. He put it in a frying pan and cooked it up and served it to the two hopeful cowboys on large plastic plates. The wilted pieces swam forlornly on the over-sized plates, as though looking for a long since departed piece of meat. The boys looked up at each other and nearly giggled in disbelief. The meagre offering was a whole lot better than nothing, but it didn't stop the growling in their bellies. Optimism prevailed, however. They fully expected to be invited to stay the night and be offered a substantial breakfast befitting weary travellers. But Jim lived up to his reputation as an oddball loner. As if on cue, he looked at his watch and said, "You boys better get going, it's getting past my bedtime."

It was now pitch dark. They bid a forlorn good-bye and headed out into surrounding night. They both stayed in the rear of the herd, as they couldn't see where they were going. They knew some of the horses had been this way before and their strategy was to follow rather than try to lead. There was a white horse in the herd, White Lady, and Donny and Keith tried to focus on her. Once in a while, they could make out her form in the gloom.

It was 12 kilometres to Harrison Flats, and they hoped the horses would lead them there. All they could do now was keep their heads down, hang on to their saddle horns and, in this fashion, weave their way down the trail. Once they reached the river, the horses were held to its course, as high clay banks hemmed them in. They followed down through the gravel beds, splashing across the river several times. Doubt about their route crept in, but the pair fought it off, hoping that the horses knew where they were going.

Eventually, they broke away from the river onto flat ground and the horses stopped to feed. From all estimates, they were where they were supposed to be. They unpacked the two packhorses, unsaddled all, and turned them loose with hobbles and bells for a well-deserved rest. The boys were now too tired to eat or even put up the tent. They rolled out their bedrolls on the ground, covered them with the tent, crawled in, and went to sleep.

Now, a cowboy's bedroll is personal, well put together, and well thought out. In those days, it was usually a big Artic Five Star sleeping bag on top of an air mattress and all of it covered and surrounded by a canvas pack tarp. Inside the sleeping bag, an inner flannel sheet and a small pillow were squirrelled away. The whole thing was rolled up like a cabbage roll and secured with a tightly tied rope. This way it was easy to lay out. All you did was untie the knot and roll it out.

They woke up in the morning with a downy quilt of snow 30 centimetres thick on top of their sleeping bags. It was a harsh world they now faced as they crawled out from under the blanket of snow. Some of their kitchen gear had been scattered about the night before and they went around kicking in the snow here and there, looking for their equipment. There was little thought of making breakfast even though they hadn't eaten anything of substance for a couple of days. Only beans remained and that didn't inspire them.

They heard some bells and, in good time, managed to catch two saddle horses and the packhorses. They led them back to camp and packed up with numb fingers, stiff tarps, and frozen lash ropes.

At last, Donny and Keith gathered up the horses and headed for the Ya Ha Tinda Ranch, depressed, wet, cold, and starving: two forlorn figures hunkered down in their wet saddles. It was easy riding down the flats for several kilometres until they crossed the river to the south and headed into the trees. From here, it was another 24 kilometres to the ranch.

By midday, the sun had come out and the snow on the ground started to melt. Steam rose from the backs of the horses, and the cowboys relished the heat from the sun. They were on a road that they had picked up near Forbidden Creek and they pushed the horses into a trot. They made good time until they neared the ranch buildings of the Ya Ha Tinda.

Here, all of a sudden, the horses stampeded. These horses had seen almost everything in a wilderness setting and grazed with the best: moose, elk, grizzly bears, but they had never seen a milk cow with a big bell around her neck. With their tails held high and to the accompaniment of snappy farts, the herd took off en masse like rifle shots. Donny and Keith rode hard to get ahead of them and slow them down. It only seemed to take minutes to cover the ground from the ranch buildings to the Big Horn Campground on the Red Deer River, a distance of three or four kilometres. It was here that Bert was supposed to meet them with fresh food.

When they got there, there was no sign of him. The horses had calmed down, so they turned them loose. It was almost dark, and they argued about whether they should set the tent up or not.

"We don't need the tent up," Donny said. "We haven't used it yet on the trip."

"We're suppose to sleep inside it not under it,"

Keith retorted. "It did snow last night you know, or did you miss that?" Keith's sarcasm prevailed and they set up the tent. It was no easy chore, as it was an old canvas wall tent that needed wooden poles and pegs. When it was all done, they sat around a big roaring fire and cursed Bert for not being there with fresh food.

Now in a foul mood, aggravated by hunger, they argued about whether to eat canned beans or hold out for Bert's arrival in the morning. That, however, was probably too optimistic. It was then that their tortured minds came up with an effective way to dispense with ever having to see the beans again. They put the cans of beans in the fire and watched them roast.

The flames licked around the cans' paper labels. The boys were getting a little bushed by now, but they were still rational and made a wise choice to step away from the fire and watch from behind some trees. The cans swelled like bloated ticks on the back of a moose. Suddenly there was a huge roar, like dynamite exploding. It was such a violent event, it blew the fire out. Donny and Keith looked at the fire, then at each other, then rolled on the ground, clutching their stomachs, laughing like hyenas. There were beans hanging off everything: trees, tents, tack, and themselves. Beans clung to their shirts and faces. It was the greatest joke they had ever pulled off. When they saw their tent, peppered and splattered in brown beans, they howled again, deep barrel-like laughter, almost choking in their mirth. They ended the evening with an improvised chicken dance around the fire as the last remnants of the coals glowed in the night.

The following morning, Donny woke up with the ridge-pole just about touching his nose, bent low under the weight of fresh snow — a good foot of it. Donny was not amused that it was always him that had to get up and build a fire. His bladder always screamed first in the morning. As he crawled out of his bedroll, Keith said smugly, "See, I told you we needed to put the tent up, Mickle."

"Yeah, yeah, you're finally right for a change."

Keith suggested they go up to the ranch house and beg for some food, but Donny quashed that idea. He wasn't quite that desperate. But he finally succumbed to hunger and managed what remained of the beans for brunch. Keith flatly refused. They were pretty testy with each other by now; it had been a tough trip and a long hunting season. All each wanted was to have a hot shower somewhere and get some decent restaurant food. They thought about trying to catch a fish in the river, but kept putting it off. Around four o'clock, Bert's arrival broke the tedium.

They ranted and raged and gave him heck,

especially Keith with his sharp, switchblade tongue. When Bert saw the brown stuff hanging from the trees and all over his tent, he gladly feigned distraction from the verbal abuse and became inquisitive. All Keith said as he climbed into the truck was, "Don't ever feed us goddamn beans again." They told him he had to buy them the biggest steak in Sundre, Alberta, and off they drove. It was two hours to Sundre on a dirt and gravel road and when they got there, as luck would have it, the restaurant was closed. They went to the bar in the hotel and started drinking beer. The only things you could get to eat in a bar back then were potato chips, peanuts, pickled eggs, pepperoni, or piggy puffs.

Though it was the end of the trip, it was not the end of their association with Jim Rimmer. They both ran into Jim a year later in the Mount Royal Hotel in Banff. They certainly didn't offer to buy him a beer. And it was a curt hello they said as they sat down some distance away. A few years later, Keith became a park warden in Jasper and Donny became a park warden in Yoho National Park.

Jim fell in the Clearwater River the following winter on his way to Indianhead warden cabin. He was on snowshoes, patrolling the district far from the cabin. It was −40°C and by the time he got to the cabin, he had severe frostbite. He lost all of his toes and parts of both feet, but it didn't stop him being a park warden. The only thing he ever complained about was that the ends on his riding boots always seemed to curl up.

Chapter 5
Stuck in the Muck

I awoke one morning to the sound of prowlers outside. I could hear movement and the rustle of tall grass and then, a muffled voice. Someone laughed — it was more like a cackle — and said, "The son-of-a-bitch is around here somewhere." Then a figure passed by the far window, wearing a cowboy hat and a plaid wool jacket. He stopped and peered in with his hand shading his eyes. It was Bert Mickle and he was cackling again. Then I heard Donny say, "Come on, Portman, open the door, we want some coffee." They were up to no good.

It was Donny's turn to feed the horses that day and

he was an early riser. Bert was visiting and came along to say hello and to see if he could catch me unawares in bed. I made some coffee and got busy getting ready for work. They took the hint, drained their cups, and went off to feed the horses. It was eight o'clock.

The sun illuminated the meadow and lingered on the backs of the horses grazing quietly on new grass. I felt inspired. It would be a fine day to take the colt out. Every year the Ya Ha Tinda ranch boss sends out young colts to learn the real work from one of the more horsewise wardens in the mountain parks, and this year I was breaking in Lane. He was a tall, spindly, black gelding who needed a lot of work because he was skittish and spooked easily at anything unfamiliar to him.

I also thought it would be a chance to go riding with Kathy Calvert, Canada's first female park warden, and assess her skill with horses. She said she had grown up with them, but that was a while ago, and people often overestimate their abilities when applying for the job. You certainly can't tell from an interview what an individual is capable of. My experience with people and horses has led me to believe it is often a patient and quiet personality, rather than a lot of exposure, that makes for success with horses.

When I returned from the warden office with Kathy, Bert and Donny were gone. I saddled her up with

Red, a reliable, stout gelding that had a great tempera-ment and was the favourite of everyone in the park. I watched her carefully as she groomed and saddled her horse without any sign of nervousness, and was reas-sured when she mounted easily. I wish I had had the same success. Lane was definitely on eggshells that day and it took patience to get saddled and mounted with-out a bucking spree. The first obstacle of the day was getting across the Trans-Canada Highway. This was one of the drawbacks of the ranch location. All the easily accessible trails were on the north side of the highway and there was no choice but to head in that direction. I reasoned that this would be good experience for Lane and there was no time like the present to get him used to the unfamiliar sights and sounds.

We crossed the highway without mishap. Kathy was obviously relishing the ride and soon we were out on the open Kicking Horse River flats — quite stunning, but rarely seen by the public. The river runs through a variety of terrain, and Lane had plenty to get used to. Red's calm approach to everything around him set the example. I decided to make it a fairly long day to work on Lane's conditioning and give him a chance to really settle down.

We stopped for lunch at a pleasant little pool and laid back to enjoy the first warm day of spring. Over sandwiches, Kathy and I talked as we watched the horses graze avidly on the lush green grass. I was feeling refreshed and confident at how the ride was going and decided we would do a little exploring on the south side of the highway on some high benches before heading home.

Again, there was no problem getting across the Trans-Canada, and soon we were working our way through a dense north-facing coniferous forest that required some negotiating. Everything came at us: small meandering streams with undercut banks, a young white-tail deer springing away in alarm, and lots of dead trees and thick willow. At times, I let Kathy take the lead, especially when we had to jump deadfall or squeeze through thick timber. Red was a pro and, since Kathy hadn't ridden in a mountain environment before, it was good for her to learn what horses could and could not handle.

It was all good experience, but soon I figured enough was enough. The bush bashing was getting tedious and it was time to go home. With this in mind, I decided to take a shorter route than the one Kathy was taking.

I rode ahead to what appeared to be an open meadow to get some relief from the bush, which was becoming oppressive. The afternoon sun slanted across the opening, making the air hazy as it shone through dust rising off old cattails. The cattails should have been the clue, but I was puzzled by the uncanny appearance of the meadow. It was grey-green, but certainly looked solid enough.

In the middle of the meadow was a large patch of perfectly flat ground. On closer inspection, it looked like a dry mud-flat, all cracked and fissured. What I didn't know was that there was a layer of water a few centimetres deep over the top. It was clear and still as glass. If I'd known this, I would not have ventured closer.

Lane blundered on in this totally unfamiliar environment, when suddenly the ground gave way and I realized we were on the edge of a swamp. The inexperienced colt had never come across ground like this, having come from the hard plains of Alberta. With little warning, he bolted forward, thinking he might just run through it, and suddenly we were well out in the middle and sinking fast.

I was just able to yell to Kathy to stay away from the swamp, but Red was too bush-wise to get into the same trouble. She looked on helplessly as I bailed off and promptly started sinking myself. Lane groaned and slipped sideways, making it difficult to get his feet under him. The slough bottom was slippery clay and mud that sucked you down. The mud held Lane's legs with ever-tightening suction and he thrashed about pathetically, trying to get his legs underneath him, but to no avail. I knew things were serious when he gave up struggling and continued to sink, now nearly completely on his side. I was up past my knees, but had hit a clay bottom and could move somewhat.

As soon as she saw our predicament, Kathy secured her horse and waded out to help. She is not very tall and by the time she reached Lane, the water was up around her thighs. There was little to do, but keep Lane's head up and try and get help for him.

I figured if we could get some poles under Lane we could prop him up until he could get out under his own steam. I left Kathy holding his head clear of the water while I waded out of the swamp and went to find what I could in the bush.

There was plenty of dead wood around and I soon returned with a few stout logs, which we jammed under the tired horse to try and lever him upright. We exhausted ourselves with this effort, but it was futile. I realized then that the only way to save him was to drag him out with more horses and ropes.

This meant one of us would have to go for help.

Since I was familiar with the country, we decided it was best if I go back to the highway to guide a rescue crew in. There was no way anyone would find us in the thick bush without help. Luckily, the radio was dry and safe in Kathy's saddlebag. I radioed out to the warden office, requesting whoever was available to load a couple of horses and head out towards Ottertail, close to where we were riding. I added, "Bring lots of rope and a gun." If we couldn't save Lane from the water, we could at least save him from an agonizingly slow death.

If Kathy heard this, she didn't say anything, but by now I realized that she would have come to the same conclusion herself. She grimaced at me as she continued to support Lane's head, saying only that I should hurry or she might sink out of sight.

I rode as quickly as I could on staunch old Red to meet Randy Robertson who had responded to the call. He had brought Elva, a solid young mare, considerable rope, and the requested rifle. Despite moving with all dispatch, it was still nearly an hour before we got back to Kathy. Lane lay perpendicular, his back facing the shore. Up to her armpits in the mud, Kathy was still stoically holding up his head, but her relief was evident. She had to be thoroughly chilled by now.

We found more poles for leverage and ran the rope out to Lane. His saddle was still in place, which provided plenty of purchase for the rope. Once the rope was rigged, Kathy remained with Lane, beating on his rump, while Randy and I drove the two pulling horses. They gave a mighty effort repeatedly, but simply could not budge him. I left Randy on shore and went to help Kathy with the poles.

Once again both horses pulled as we tried to force Lane to his feet. He tried valiantly to stand up and get his feet under him, but the mud held him fast on his side like an insect on flypaper. Lane would have to give us all the help he could, if we were to get him out. But he was both exhausted and demoralized with the effort. We tried again and this time, poor Elva foundered on the shore. We stopped then to give everyone a break. I was getting more and more desperate, truly afraid I would have to use the rifle.

Lane began to struggle again; then slowly, his angle started to improve, getting more and more in line with the shore. Finally he got one leg under his chest. We got the pulling horses back in position. At that point, Red looked back and to this day I believe I detected a look of pity — and then of resolve. He momentarily nuzzled Elva, then both heaved mightily on the ropes, while we pushed and beat on Lane. He thrust forward with a huge effort and suddenly he was free, up and lunging toward the shore. I thought he would never stop. He bolted out of the swamp as though it were on fire. If he hadn't been held by the rope, he probably would have run all way to the north confines of the park.

Randy laughed as Kathy fell back in the swamp, worn out by the effort. We watched Lane as he stood there trembling and then exhaled deeply through his nose. With a nervous energy, he started to feed on the tender grasses, as if he were trying to put the awful experience behind him. The rope was coiled and the rifle packed away before we rode quietly back to the ranch.

To this day, I have never forgotten the feeling of empathy the rescue horses seemed to have for Lane. He was just a colt and they knew he was close to losing his life. Although we had done everything we could for the horse, it was the valiant efforts of Elva and Red that saved him in the end.

Chapter 6
The Swinging Bridge

A couple of good friends, Art Twomey and Margie Jamieson, decided to undertake an ambitious pack trip along the Continental Divide with some mules and a saddle horse each. They set out from Canal Flats, British Columbia, and planned to use the summer months to make it as far as Mt. Sir Alexander, a remote and fascinating area north of Mt. Robson. It was a three-month journey that would take them through some of the most spectacular country Banff and Jasper National Parks had to offer.

Part of their journey led them east of the Icefield Parkway (the Banff–Jasper Highway) into the remote

Siffleur Wilderness. En route, they restocked in Banff, then headed north, across the Red Deer River and up the Clearwater River to a nice campsite below Devon Lakes.

My wife, Kathy, and I had previously arranged to meet Art and Margie here with a couple of packhorses loaded with fresh supplies. We set out from Lake Louise up the Pipestone, intending to get to Devon Lakes over the Pipestone and Clearwater passes. On the way up the Pipestone, we ran across a couple of Swiss gentlemen leading two horses that had riding saddles on them. Two large packs hung from the saddle horns. The packs were rearranged on to one animal whenever they had to ride the other across the rivers they encountered. They negotiated some substantial river crossings this way without getting wet.

These boys were living their dream of travelling through the Canadian Rockies with horses. They had bought two broken down sorrels from a less-than-honest farmer around Calgary and had somehow made it from Banff to Lake Louise knowing very little about horses. They intended to travel all the way to Jasper, more or less via the same route as Art and Margie. When we met them, they had already been informed by the Banff warden service that the horses could not be tied up all night, that they needed to graze and recoup their energy.

The author on the banks of the Porcupine Lake inlet,
Siffleur Wilderness

I asked them how they were managing with the
horses and they gave me a rather puzzled look,
shrugged their shoulders, and said they were getting by.
I gathered from their broken English that at night they
would turn one horse loose to graze while the other
remained tied up. At about midnight they would switch
the animals and, in that fashion, the horses were fed
and remained in close proximity to their camp.

We left them and continued our journey north and east to meet Art and Margie at Devon Lakes. Besides fresh food, we also had the camping permits they needed to get through to Jasper with.

The campsite below Devon Lakes is one of the most tranquil and peaceful spots around. It is located next to a lush meadow, well suited for horses with an inviting campsite at the edge of a dark, spruce forest. The location is open with flat level ground and a convenient brook that gurgles cheerfully nearby.

Art and Margie were in camp when we arrived and were well rested, as they had got there the previous day. They had their teepee up and a small fire going. They greeted us warmly and helped us unload the packhorses. Soon, we were settled down by the fire, while the horses grazed nearby. They filled us in on their trip, and Art showed us the several pan-size trout he had caught at Devon Lakes. He prepared them with herbs and spices and wrapped each individually in tin foil. They were soon sizzling away in the open fire.

Kathy and I had brought some fiddlehead greens and rice with us, plus a bottle of white wine, which complimented the fish nicely. Afterwards we relaxed around the fire telling stories and catching up on each other's lives. We took notice of the two Swiss men who showed up at dusk, still leading their horses. They camped a good distance away from us, seeming to want their privacy. It suited us fine.

We spent the next day in leisurely fashion, exploring the surrounding area and catching a few more fish. They added greatly to the wholesome breakfast we prepared for ourselves the following morning before breaking camp.

We intended to travel another day with our friends before leaving them to their northern journey. The ride to the pass and over to the Siffleur River was spectacular under deep blue skies that silhouetted the jagged peaks. As we travelled down the Siffleur Valley, snaking across the river in many places, we felt we had the land all to ourselves. We had left the Swiss behind, as they were having an extra layover day, allowing the two parties to gain some distance between each other.

We got to Isabella Lake early that afternoon, foregoing camp in lieu of a pleasant warden cabin. That evening, Art and I, wearing shorts and running shoes, waded across a deep channel to the other side of Isabella Lake. Rainbow trout often lurked on a shallow shelf on this side.

The lake can be difficult to fish in the first half of the summer. It clouds over with silt, washed down from melting glaciers. The silt creates the opaque, turquoise colour seen in many mountain lakes in the early summer. Later in the summer, it clears to a deep, crystal blue, making for great fishing. The water was cool, but we soon forgot about that as we concentrated on fishing for trout.

On this particular evening, the water was as smooth as glass right across the lake. The trout began to rise and feed on the surface insects just as we arrived. Art had his fly rod out and assembled in a matter of minutes and soon he had a splashing rainbow near at hand, slapping water all over his torso and face. It was a big one and it was putting on a real display. Art played it for quite awhile before expertly coaxing the fish into the landing net.

It took a little longer for me to get my collapsible rod together and my reel in place, but soon enough, I had my spinner on — a red and white, size eight, Len Thompson. The shelf was six or seven metres away and I cast diagonally across it and well beyond, working it back slowly, just enough to give the spoon adequate action. As the lure crossed the line of dark vegetation that marked the shelf, there was a sudden hit on the line. A substantial amount of wiggling resonated up the rod. I played the fish for quite some time, then started to reel it in.

We fished like this until we had caught two each. The sound of our splashing, laughter, and light banter carried easily on the smooth surface of the lake. The girls could hear us plainly a kilometre away as they sat and read in the angled beam of the evening sun. Behind them, the cabin had taken on a rich and oily texture. It flashed continually across the lake, like a beacon, illuminated by the slanting sunlight. When the sun went behind the mountain and dusk settled over the landscape we returned to the cabin: shivering, cold, and ready for a hearty fish dinner.

Kathy and I said goodbye to Art and Margie the next morning. They were continuing their journey north down the Siffleur River to where it finally enters the Saskatchewan River at the Kootenay Plains. We were heading over Dolomite Pass, to the trailhead at Crowfoot Lookout near Bow Lake on the Icefield Parkway.

Our trip out was uneventful, broken only by the welcome transition from rock-strewn fields to the expanse of alpine meadows and blue lakes scooped out by long-receded glaciers. Once we broke through a crack in the rock at the top of Dolomite Pass, we caught sight of the highway in the distance. Helen Lake, far below, oval and serene with its velvet green shoulders, urged us on.

Art and Margie meanwhile continued down through the deep forest of the mid-Siffleur until they reached Bert Mickle's old hunting camp. From here they followed an old seismic line that eventually deposited them among green grass and aspen stands that make up much of the Kootenay Plains periphery. When they hit the Saskatchewan River, they were taken aback by its size and colour. It no longer carried the silt of melting glaciers. It was cleaner and much bluer.

The Saskatchewan is not an easy river to cross in August as it is wide, swift, and deep. Entering and exiting is straightforward, as it has no sharp drops along its bank in this section. However, once in the water the horses are committed to swimming almost the whole width of the river. It seems forever before the horses' feet start to hit bottom again. Some never learn how to swim properly and others have so little buoyancy, they almost walk along the bottom.

The Swiss pair had taken the same route and soon met up with Art and Margie again. The river is notoriously tough to cross, and both Art and Margie were worried about how the two men, boys really, would manage with their dubious horses.

There is a long, swinging suspension bridge for foot traffic, just wide enough for hikers, right at the river crossing. The bridge is made of spaced wooden planks, with gaps just wide enough to fit a wayward foot. Our friends carried all their boxes and duffel across the bridge — time consuming and hard work, but it allowed the mules to swim the river safely, unencumbered with heavy packs. Margie had never crossed such a large river with her mare before and decided to swim the river with her and the mules.

Just as they got into the current, Margie realized her horse couldn't swim. Before she could react, Margie was upside down and sinking fast beneath her saddle horse. Usually in this situation, if the horse is having trouble swimming, it is best to get off and catch the horse's tail if possible. This way the horse will pull you across to the far shore. But for Margie, there was no horse to hang on to. She got back to the near shore just in time to see the mare float down the river under the bridge. To her relief, the horse washed up on the same side as she did, a considerable distance downstream from where they started. The mules were better at this endeavour and crossed with ease, emerging eventually on the other side. Art was there to meet them, but was now concerned for Margie and her horse. How would they ever entice the horse back into the river and get her to the far shore?

The two boys had arrived just in time to see the spectacle and had no intention of repeating it. They had seen the size of the river and the swinging bridge, and watched as horse and rider foundered in the rushing water. After considering their options, they decided to walk their two horses across the slatted bridge. To Art's astonishment, the horses complacently negotiated the swaying, bouncing bridge as though they were veterans of a three-ring circus act.

Margie's horse, now thoroughly alarmed at the prospect of having to swim again, saw this solution and decided it was the only way to go. Before they knew it, the mare joined the other two and nimbly crossed the bridge behind them. The boys and the three horses all arrived safe and sound on the other side. A wet and bedraggled Margie soon joined them.

This is not the recommended way to get your horses across the river at Kootenay Plains. In fact, it would be almost impossible to get a horse to repeat the stunt suspended high above the Saskatchewan River. For the Swiss, ignorance was bliss, and for Art and Margie, it would be one of many memorable highlights on a remarkable trip along the Continental Divide.

Chapter 7
The Eccentric Jim Rimmer

Perry Jacobson grew up immersed in ranching life. His parents originally had a spread near Medicine Hat, Alberta. Then, when he was 16 years old, they moved to the Millarville area. They bought the old Millar place, which was quite famous at the time. The ranch had been established between 1883 and 1885 and many of the original buildings were still standing. Perry was into rodeo as a youth and spent much of his free time going to different events as a roper. In the fall, the family would set out for the nearby mountains with their pack-horses and do some hunting.

Although Perry had a strong background with horses and rodeo, he was also a good student in school and eventually went on to university. His real passion, however, was for the outdoors and doing what he loved best — riding horses. So, it was no surprise that he was attracted to the warden service as a line of work and certainly no surprise that he got hired on. Perry became a seasonal warden in 1972 in Banff National Park — part of a new wave of young wardens with a post-secondary education. One of Perry's early assignments was to help out Jim Rimmer who was stationed at Saskatchewan River Crossing. Jim, by contrast, was an "old school" warden and very set in his ways.

That summer, Jim had no seasonal warden assigned to help him out. Every time he came to Lake Louise, he would complain to his boss that he was getting no help. On one particular occasion, he wanted to go up the Howse River and collect the winter's supply of firewood. Perry was the low man on the totem pole then and was selected to go.

Jim's reputation preceded him.

Larry Gilmar, Perry's boss, had already regaled Perry with many stories about the eccentric Englishman. Perry didn't mind going; he was looking forward to meeting Jim and getting to know him better. As Perry was preparing to depart, Larry suddenly blurted out —

like a long overdue confession — that if it got too rough out there, he should just come home.

As things would have it, Jim was in a bad mood when the two met. After brief introductions, Jim and Perry went down to the corral to get the horses ready. Perry was looking forward to getting out and away from the office. He had no idea what his role would be, but he thought that with his horse experience, he would be on more or less equal terms. Perry went to catch his horse.

"No, no, no, you can't do that," Jim commanded. "You just watch me."

"I'm quite comfortable with horses. I was raised on a ranch."

"Well, well" Jim said in his English accent, "we'll see about that." Perry didn't want to cause any trouble, so he sat back and watched.

He watched Jim stroll into the corral among the horses. A lariat twirled around his head like a ground-tied helicopter desperately trying to lift off. The horses stampeded counter clockwise around him in a cloud of dust, hugging the inside of the railed fence. The faster he twirled the rope, the harder they ran. After rousing the horses to a frenzy, Jim put the rope aside and waited among the swirling clouds of dust for the horses to settle down. It took the longest time, but finally they all came to a stop, their backs up against the railed fence, their eyes bulging with alarm as they eyed Jim in the centre of the corral. Perry quietly caught his horse and, without a word, left the corral to Jim and his unusual antics.

Eventually, the horses were saddled, and then it was time to pack the boxes with their food and duffel.

"Did you bring your food?"

"Yeah," said Perry. "I went and bought supplies through the government."

"Huh," Jim said, "I don't do that. I go on my own rations."

Perry offered to help pack up the horses, but Jim would have nothing to do with that. He instructed Perry to stand back, while he made sure they were packed to his liking. Now, the diamond made by the lash ropes on a packhorse is supposed to be positioned on the top of the pack in the middle, but because Jim was trying too hard to get a tight diamond, he pulled it well over to one side. Perry decided to let it be and not say anything, as Jim seemed so touchy about accepting any help. He seemed to have little regard for Perry's capabilities.

Perry watched as Jim tailed the packhorses in a string. Perry offered to lead a packhorse, making it easier for Jim, but the man wanted nothing to do with that notion, either. Jim tied the halter-shank of one packhorse to the tail of another, but unwittingly left the rope between them too long. There was two to three metres of slack, and Perry pointed this out to Jim.

"My ponies are all right, you'll see," was all he said. And with that they headed out, followed closely by Jim's dog, Spook, a white English bullterrier.

They arrived at the Mistaya River. The water was high after the recent rains and laden with big boulders which rolled along the bottom and made for a treacherous crossing. It was "bobbing water," which means the water level was well past the horses' bellies.

Jim barged into the river leading the packhorses, giving them little chance to anticipate how they were going to negotiate the crossing. Spook jumped in upstream of the horses, and was immediately swept away by the current. Despite his panicky doggie paddling, he was being carried down towards the horses. He was struggling madly just above the last packhorse before he was swept up against it, then disappeared under the horse's belly, only to pop up on the other side. Away he went, bobbing on the waves like a sailor, as Jim yelled "Swim for it Spook, swim for it." Spook was swept all the way down to where the Mistaya runs into the Saskatchewan River — almost a kilometre. He came out on the far shore, but he just about drowned. When he caught up to the rest of the group, the dog took off like a shot. Jim spent the rest of the day yelling, "Here Spook, where are you Spook?" but the dog was long gone.

In the meantime, the packhorse that Spook had been swept under had come unglued and when they reached the far shore, he jumped ahead and stepped right over the halter shank. Jim was oblivious to all this, thinking only of his dog as he receded from view. The horse hopped along trying to keep up, and Perry finally yelled at Jim to stop. Once he got Jim's attention, he stopped, climbed off his saddle horse and got the packstring straightened out. Around this time, the nearly-drowned Spook finally showed up, much to Jim's relief.

They got up the trail about three kilometres when Bog, the last packhorse, stepped over the rope again. Bog pulled back immediately, stopping the packhorse ahead of him, whose tail was being yanked on with great gusto. This, in turn, halted the packhorse Jim was leading. Jim had fastened a loop at the end of the packhorse's halter-shank and dropped it over his saddle horn. This is something you never do if you want to stay alive working around horses. The halter-shank from the packhorse Jim was leading was now firmly secured to Jim's saddle, making it impossible to release when the horse pulled back. When this happened, Jim suddenly found himself and his saddle horse perpendicular to the pack string.

By now, Bog was in a state of real terror, pulling

back and bucking as the pack on his back started to fall apart. With all the packhorses now pulling back madly, neither Jim nor Cindy, his saddle horse, had a chance. Down they went in a cloud of dust, as Perry gaped in horror at the unfolding wreck. When Cindy went down, the rope came off the saddle horn and the packhorses all flew backwards into a giant heap.

In the blink of an eye, Perry flicked his knife and cut the rope between the two packhorses and the still-standing Bog. Bog immediately took off, dragging ropes, pack tarps, and boxes behind him. Perry managed to get the other two packhorses up on their feet and checked on Jim, who was stunned and dishevelled. Once he realized Jim was unhurt, Perry headed off to retrieve Bog and the scattered gear. He would have to watch Jim very closely from here on in if he wanted to survive this trip.

They finally got things sorted out and Perry asked if he could lead him now.

"You can lead him now." No argument there. When they got to the Howse Cabin, Perry looked after the horses, while Jim went inside to light the stove. Just before going in Jim commented, "I noticed you're not too bad with horses. You can unsaddle them."

Perry stood by the hitching rail at the front of the cabin, happy with this new-found recognition. He could see Jim through the open doorway. There was an old four-lid stove in the cabin and he was pouring white gas onto the logs as a starter for the fire. Perry watched this, and was thinking it was a terrible lot of white gas to be putting on the wood when Jim struck the match. He threw the match in the stove and suddenly there was a huge KABOOM! Flames engulfed Jim where he stood. All the lids blew out of the stove, levitating in midair for a split second, one lid carrying on up to hit the ceiling. It was a flat white ceiling, and the lid hit with a forceful "thwang," leaving a perfect black circle. Down they all came, crashing and clattering as Jim came out of the cabin slapping at his eyebrows. He turned around, pale with ash, the hair around his face totally singed, and said, "Tea will be ready in a minute."

Now, they had come up the valley to get some wood in and that's what they put their minds to in the ensuing days. Jim was planning lots of winter snowshoeing trips and would need the firewood.

They went off into the bush and found a spot with plenty of dead standing timber, including a large spruce. That one was going to be a chore to skid to the cabin. Perry had worked in the logging industry as a faller for several years and asked Jim if he wanted him to fall the trees.

"No," Jim replied, "you just stand back and watch."

"I know how to fall trees," Perry said. But Jim told

him just to watch and observe.

Jim had tied old Barney about 16 or 20 metres from where he was cutting the big spruce. Perry noticed from the way Jim had notched the tree that it was going to fall on top of the horse. He went over to Jim and pointed out that the tree was notched to fall on Barney.

"No, it's fine," Jim said abruptly. Perry was persistent and Jim continued, "All right, move the old bastard if it's going to make you feel better." So with that Perry moved Barney. Sure as anything, after jamming the chainsaw a few times, Jim brought the old spruce down with a crash. It wiped out the entire area where the horse had been standing.

When the dust settled, Jim looked over at Perry and said, "It's a good thing we moved that horse."

The pair spent five days cutting wood, and every day brought another event. The trees were big and they bucked them up into one or two metre lengths. Normally, you would skid logs using a horse, but Jim had other plans.

Jim planned to pack the logs to the cabin on old Barney, one on each side of the horse. This was a huge load for the horse, but Perry's protests fell on deaf ears. When Jim made up his mind, nothing would change it.

They tried to pack thick green logs, almost two metres long and half the diameter of a 45 gallon drum, on either side of the horse like two pack boxes. But because the logs were so heavy and unwieldly, it took both of them to work on one side at a time. It was a tricky manoeuvre, because once one side was secure, it was imperative to tie up the other side before the weight of the first log pulled the saddle over. If not done quickly enough, the saddle would roll and all hell could break loose.

They were struggling with the weight of the second log, when Barney started to jump around, forcing them to follow, all the while trying to hold up the weight. As Perry recounted later, "We tried to roll this goddamn log on the side of the horse. It was at least five feet long and we were busting a gut trying to get this thing up there, when all of a sudden there was this huge fart." A branch on the log they were trying to load must have poked Barney in the ribs. The horse gave off a long, drawn-out fart that scared him as much as the logs did, and he was gone. The men both stood there, exasperated, watching the horse make good his escape, when suddenly, Jim disappeared. He was there one minute and the next, he was following the horse feet first with a basket rope looped around his foot.

Jim got acquainted with some serious bush, undergrowth, and deadfall in his travels behind the horse. Perry tried to follow as best he could, but riding boots are not designed for sprinting. After a long time, the rope came unravelled from Jim's foot and he came to rest in a heap at the base of a towering Engelmann spruce.

It took Perry about five minutes to catch Barney, about the time it took Jim to regain consciousness. Unbelievably, he hadn't broken anything. Jim moved very slowly and softly for a few days after that, but soon returned to his cranky old self.

During the time Jim convalesced, they continued to work at bringing in the wood. And as Perry said, "these wild events went on and on with frequent regularity." During this period, Jim went into a deep depression. He talked little and spent his quiet time alone reading a book, which suited Perry just fine.

The cabin was partitioned, separating the bedroom from the kitchen, which allowed the pair their own personal space: Perry had the kitchen, and Jim the bedroom. It was only at night when they were asleep or when they ate a meal together that they shared the same room. At times Jim would go into a black mood and stop speaking altogether.

Jim used to suffer from bad asthma attacks. He had this little tube with a propeller on it that he used to suck on. Lying in bed on the only other army cot in the back room, Jim would suck on it so hard, Perry imagined he could almost hover.

Before long, Perry noticed that the dog often slept on Jim's chest at night. Spook wasn't a big dog, but he was heavy and this couldn't have helped Jim's asthma. The white dog rose and fell on Jim's chest in the moonlight, and every time Jim breathed in, a sort of whizzing sound came out of him, followed by the sound of air escaping a slowly deflating tire. It kept Perry awake for hours.

Another peculiarity that Jim had was never hobbling his horses.

"Don't these horses ever pull out?" Perry said one day. You always had to phrase things as a question with Jim if you expected to get a decent explanation and not have a fight on your hands.

"No, no." He said, "my ponies like me. They'll be here. Don't you worry."

Well, each day they were found farther and farther from the cabin. One morning, Jim left at 7:00 a.m. with a bridle in his hand and a small sack of oats to catch the horses. By 11:00 a.m. he hadn't returned and Perry was concerned. Around noon, he heard a racket and saw the horses come careening around the corner. Perry scampered out and caught them and put them in the corral. Considering Jim's track record, Perry saddled his horse, figuring Jim might be in trouble.

Perry headed out on his saddle horse in the

direction of the river. He met Jim not far from the cabin. He was wearing hip waders, the ones the pack rats had chewed holes in. Crossing the river in the awkward things, he had fallen in, filling them to the brim with water. He squished with every step, and small fountains squirted out through the holes.

They got back to the cabin and packed up and were soon on the trail again, heading for Saskatchewan Crossing. By the time they got on the trail, Jim was happy. You could always tell when Jim was having a good day by the unusual tune he would sing, over and over again. Similar to the ring of a bell, a strong "d" was followed by an ever weakening "eee," then a few seconds later another "deee."

When they got to the Crossing and stepped off their horses, Jim was indeed in a good mood and he looked over at Perry and said, "By God, we make a pretty good team." It never occurred to Perry that they made a good team. "I'll get some photographs of the trip developed for you," Jim added.

"Yeah, I noticed you've been taking some pictures," said Perry.

"Yes, I document all my trips, you know."

Perry saw Jim about a month later and asked if he ever got his pictures back.

"What pictures?" Jim asked.

"Well, up the Howse River, of course."

"Oh, those," he said. "Hmm, I had the damn lens cap on the whole time. Didn't get any of the trip."

Chapter 8
Trailing Horses from the Ya Ha Tinda

One of the more thrilling events of the year for many park wardens happens in the spring when all the horses return from the Ya Ha Tinda for the summer's work. The event heralded the coming of the season and long days full of excitement and adventure associated with looking after a national park in the Canadian Rockies. Ya Ha Tinda is the name of the government ranch located west of Sundre, on the sunny eastern slopes of the mountains. Here, the horses spend the winter, surviving on the open range. In past years, the horses were brought back by truck, but that all changed when Banff National Park hired a new chief park warden who enjoyed riding and getting out in the backcountry. Gaby Fortin was from Quebec and, with typical French-Canadian passion, embraced all that was western about horses and the associated lifestyle.

He reasoned it would be good to trail the horses back through the park once the passes were free of snow and the trails were open. It was a bonding exercise for the staff and helped settle the horses into the idea of going back to work again. Fresh off the range, the horses were full of vim and vigour. The distance was long, which made for a gruelling trip for the first ride of the year. Muscles and backsides accustomed to softer truck seats over the winter took the brunt of the load.

Not just anyone was asked to go. In fact, only those with experience were considered and being asked was a privilege. When Gaby Fortin decided to trail the horses, he felt it wouldn't be worthwhile unless the Kootenay and Yoho horses were included as well. Diplomatically, one person from each park was asked along. Usually, it was the barn boss or an experienced senior warden.

I was pleased when Gaby offhandedly asked if I'd be interested in going one spring. I had considerable experience with horses, having worked for Parks Canada in Jasper, Banff, and Yoho national parks. Even though I had the background, it was nice to get the recognition and be singled out for the trip. I suppressed my excitement around the warden office, knowing I could let it all out when I got home to tell my wife. She would understand.

Kathy was a park warden working in Yoho National Park, just across the provincial border from Lake Louise where we lived. It was a good arrangement. We didn't have to work in the same park and the drive from Lake Louise to the boundary of Yoho was only eight kilometres. Kathy had also worked around horses and was a good rider, as well as an experienced backcountry traveller. I knew she would be really happy for me and congratulate me for the opportunity it was.

She appeared to be as thrilled as I was. Of course, she wanted to know who was going from Yoho, and was not surprised to hear it was Earl Hayes, the barn boss. Earl was an old hand with horses and had worked in Yoho for the past few years. He kept the string in good order and passed on his considerable experience and sound direction to all the new wardens in need of coaching. Kathy had worked closely with him in Yoho and had been given a young horse of her own to work with the previous year. It was worthy of her capabilities and she was proud of her success with the filly. I tried not to gloat too much when I told her the details of the trip, but I saw the envy in her eyes.

A couple of days went by. I got my gear in order and

downplayed the details with Kathy. I sensed more envy each passing day. But one day Kathy came home looking for all the world like she had just won the lottery. In a sense, she had. She waltzed in, beaming gleefully. Unwittingly shattering my happiness, she announced "You'll never guess what happened! Earl has to go to a wedding and can't make the trip. My boss said I could go instead!" She chattered away, not noticing my silent astonishment.

"No one else is at work that can handle that type of ride," she added. "Gord said there was no alternative, so I'm getting my stuff together tonight. It'll be great!"

I wasn't speechless for long. I stared at her as though she was demented and uttered a string of oaths that even I thought I'd left behind on the trail. How could she do this? I get the rare opportunity to go on a trip that is the envy of many in the warden service, a chance to be with the boys, chase horses across the country, drink whisky, and tell tales into the wee hours.

And I had to take my wife!

It was insupportable! I sat down with a thud, wondering what had happened to my perfect world. How could I face the guys and tell them my wife was coming? Why couldn't I have married a teacher or a nurse?

I decided the best defense was offense. I derided her. I told her I wouldn't go if she was going. That was it.

I wouldn't go and she would feel so bad, she would be forced to back out. Hell, they didn't need anyone from Yoho. They only had 13 horses anyway.

This tactic didn't get the results I wanted. She just said it was too bad I would miss such a good trip on her account, but Yoho must be represented and she was going and that was that. This really set me back: I didn't want to back out. My only choice now was to ignore her, pretend she didn't exist. The last thing I wanted was for the guys to think I had something to do with her going. That definitely needed to be made clear to all involved. I said she would have to find her own way there and to forget about me having anything to do with her on the trip.

Very quickly, the much-anticipated day approached. It turned out that our neighbour, Dale Loewen, was also going and we had discussed the trip together on a few occasions. Well aware of his participation, Kathy went next door and arranged to drive to the Banff barns with Dale early the following morning. It was a somber night for me, made even more miserable by the fact that my wife, selfishly, seemed not to understand my predicament. She was up-beat and excited about the impending adventure, chatting merrily away with my turncoat neighbour.

In the gloom of the early morning, two warden trucks pulled out of Lake Louise for Banff. I drove in suppressed anger by myself, trailing the other two in their truck. I caught their reflection in the headlights as they talked animatedly. I secretly hoped Kathy would regret going once things came down to the crunch and she had to keep up with the boys.

Kathy still had to explain to Gaby why she was there and not Earl. That would be interesting. I envisioned her being told to go home. Then I figured, no, she would get bucked off and have to be taken out by air ambulance, an evil thought I quickly suppressed. Maybe she would just get scared and apologize to everyone, especially me, and then go home. I was even beginning to congratulate myself on my restraint. I had certainly tried to warn her what she was up against.

I didn't want to miss Kathy's arrival and had long since passed Dale as he dawdled to Banff. I arrived early at the barns before the sun was up, and found the place in organized chaos. Transportation to Ya Ha Tinda was being arranged and gear and people accounted for as last minute plans were tailored to the day. This was all being done under the guidance and supervision of Banff's barn boss, Johnny Nylund.

After some delay, Dale and Kathy arrived. If Gaby was surprised to see her, he didn't show it. He casually asked her where Earl was. As she hauled out her saddle, she simply said that he had to go to a wedding, adding that her Chief Park Warden asked her to fill in instead. Well, obviously my fall-back strategy hadn't worked. Maybe she would still get scared and go home, but by now I didn't think that would work either. Nobody said a thing to me — no reference to our relationship, no question about her being there at all.

The trip would take three days as 10 wardens herded 120 head of wild, range horses over Snow Creek Summit, down the Cascade Fire Road to the Banff Government Barns, at that time located just past the airstrip. The distance was roughly 90 kilometres. The tricky part would be getting the horses off the range, which they had grown accustomed to and would not want to leave.

The whole trip would be a test of endurance and riding skills, trying to keep up with the herd and moving them without losing any on the way. From past experience chasing wild horses in the foothills in my younger days, I knew we would constantly be heading them off. They would be trying to circle back home through territory they knew much better than many of us did. It would be a wild ride for anyone who had not done this sort of thing before.

When we arrived at the Ya Ha Tinda Ranch our first test that morning was to catch a mount suitable to the task. When the ranch hands had brought the horses in, they had been able to keep the ones belonging to each park separate. That way we could ride a mount we knew. This was important, because you wanted to know what you were getting in terms of stamina and temperament for the chase ahead. No one needed a bronc or a horse that couldn't keep up. I had worked in Yoho for several years before moving to Banff and knew those horses pretty well — better, in fact, than I knew the Banff horses. I don't think Kathy really cared or was surprised when I chose one of the finest horses from the Yoho string for the coming days.

She was a fine, tall mare with lots of fire and spirit, appropriately called Flirt. I knew Kathy had her own personal favourite and, when she claimed him, I was just a little apprehensive, because he could be a handful. His name was Charcoal and, as Kathy had often reminded me, he looked like a smaller version of Fury from the old television series of the same name. According to Kathy, he was as wild as a wolf after a winter on the range and he put on quite a show at being caught. To me, he had the potential to buck her off.

One of the cowboys trying to get a rope on him finally looked at Kathy and said, "Are you sure this is the one you want?" She was sure. She had ridden him a lot under all kinds of conditions, particularly in Yoho's year-end gymkhana events, where you really got to know what a horse could do. He was a sure-footed, fast little quarter horse and arguably the best in the park. It was a good choice, and I had to admit it wasn't likely she was going home unless he bucked her off. That was something I was starting to get concerned about. I was still mad, though, and when she threw her saddle on him, I couldn't resist saying loudly, "Better be careful getting on. Remember, he dumped you last year when you were mounting." All eyes fell on me as I read their minds. They wondered why I wasn't topping the mare off for her. This meant riding the horse first to get the buck out of her. I said nothing: my body language said it all.

Every cowboy and warden in spitting distance stopped what they were doing to see if there was going to be a show. I almost felt sorry for Kathy, when she looked at the row of men waiting to see if she would pass the first test. It was no time to screw up and I had pretty well declared I wasn't in her camp. But she kept her cool, and I began to remember why I married her.

"Yeah, thanks for reminding me," she calmly replied. "I better walk him some to get him settled down." She headed off for a quiet place where she could work the horse alone and not be distracted by the commotion. She was also probably looking for a stump as she wasn't very tall—a problem when you are mounting a jumpy horse that hasn't been ridden in eight months.

Everyone got busy, then, as there was still a lot to do, and the herd was getting restless. Nobody really noticed when Kathy quietly showed up, mounted and ready to ride. And what a ride! We had 120 head of horses to chase 27 kilometres to Scotch Camp, our first destination, across open country full of bush, potholes, ditches, logs, and anything else that popped up. The herd was wild and full of energy, and most of the ride would be at a flat out run. At any point, the herd could try to double back or break away, and it was our job to head them off. You could never watch your own mount, as your eyes had to be trained on the fleeing animals to anticipate their every move. Sometimes you might wind up going full blast through a dense stand of trees where low lying branches could sweep you off. But once down, you could never catch up. It was critical to trust your mount to keep his feet and choose the best ground.

Cal Hayes, the diminutive ranch foreman, had a glint in his eye as he mounted the corral railing.

"Are you ready?" he shouted. "Here they come!"

The gates swung open and the chase was on. Off we went with Johnny Nylund and Larry Gilmar leading the herd. We were all caught off guard as we madly tried to get in position to get them around the first corner and headed in the right direction. It all seemed to happen so quickly. My horse was flying over the ground, pounding up the turf as we hazed a small group of Kootenay horses back to the trail. Out of the corner of my eye, I could see Kathy as she cleared a ditch, chasing a small bay. She was grinning from ear to ear as she waved at one of the cowboys helping her with a few of the more independent horses. He was grinning back, but from then on, no one paid her any special attention. She was a full part of the crew and that was all that counted now that we were on our way.

From the get-go, Johnny and Larry were at a full gallop, trying to keep ahead of the pent-up mass of energy. They were concerned about being overtaken by some of the faster animals and losing their position as leader, where they could control the direction the herd would take. They rode hard, waving their arms, yelling, keeping the attention of the horses at the front on them and not on the open terrain ahead. The last thing that Johnny and Larry needed was for the riders at the back to push the horses too much or crowd them. This would put pressure on the herd. They needn't have worried: everyone was riding pell-mell just to keep up.

Larry was an older, wily veteran of the warden service who was quite stocky in build. He was amazingly agile for a man his size and had reflexes as quick as a cat. He was the type of guy who, if you hung him from a rooftop by his boot straps, would always land on his feet.

Johnny was one of the boys from Millarville, well suited for his present position at the head of the line. When Cal Hayes retired as the ranch boss at the Ya Ha Tinda, Johnny would be selected by Gaby to fill the void. He was eminently assisted by his wife Marie, as capable a woman as any working around horses and helping her husband with the intricacies of running a ranch with a breeding program.

On we went, mile after bone-jarring mile, ducking and jumping whatever came our way. Soon the wranglers were working as a team and after 20 kilometres we were able to set a steady pace to the cabin.

Scotch Camp is one of the more beautifully situated warden cabins in Banff National Park. It sits at the base of the eastern mountains overlooking the meadows and river flats of the Red Deer River. It was an excellent place to hold the horses for the night before the trek over Snow Creek Summit. The grazing was good and it was familiar territory to most of the herd.

Kathy knew most of the other wardens on the trip and was settling in quite comfortably to help out with camp chores. My refusal to acknowledge her presence was getting a bit uncomfortable for me, but not at all for her. In fact, she ignored me altogether. If anyone thought this odd, nobody said a word. Before long the cook had steaks and beans ready for the crew. The food and beer mellowed the tired riders and soon we were reflecting on how well the day had gone. Everyone had a story of catching strays, clearing bush, or surviving a nasty jump. Before long I was passing comments Kathy's way. Maybe my concerns about having a wife along were misplaced. By the time I rolled up for bed, it was as though there had never been an argument about her coming on this trip.

The next day took us over Snow Creek Summit on the old Cascade Fire Road that used to service all the warden cabins from Banff through to Scotch Camp. The road runs through some of the most beautiful country on the eastern slopes of the Rockies, but the road was soon to be closed for rehabilitation. This is prime grizzly bear country and the road was no longer needed as a fire access with the advent of the helicopter.

The horses were not particularly eager to keep going in the direction of Banff, but the country was more confined and it was difficult for them to make a break through the timber. They were also tired from the run the previous day and were less inclined to revolt. That wouldn't last when we came to the open meadows of the summit. We were ready for them and when we hit the high meadows, the herd was well flanked with a lead rider ahead to give direction. I rode to the side where I liked to be, apart and on my own to handle strays trying to sneak back through the bush. I had experience in deep timber and knew how to bring them back. It was a fine day; the sun shone on the newly budding willows, and there was plenty of dew on the grass. The horses cut a swath through the scrub as they let fly over the summit.

Day two ended at Windy warden cabin, on the Panther River. We had covered only 16 kilometres on the second day, because the climb to the summit was hard on the horses. We also had to watch out for their feet, which were not shod. The evening meal was quiet that night: the big push would be on the final day to Banff.

The next morning held the same excitement as the first day, if anything could equal that. We expected a long ride and many of the guys were using new horses for this last push. Not to my surprise, Kathy chose to ride her filly from the year before. She had been building a bond with the young horse and felt that this was the best way to re-establish that connection for the coming summer.

I agreed with her, but I knew she was taking a chance. The filly had little experience with chasing horses and the last lap of the day would be a chase across the open-air strip to the government barns. But I had complete faith in Kathy's abilities and by now I was 100 per cent behind her decision to join the trip. So I was a little surprised when one of the older wardens asked me if I wanted to ride the filly in the corral first to top her off. I realized that it was vital for Kathy to have a chance to show her independence and prove her capabilities. I managed to look surprised and said, "Hell, it's her horse, let her do it."

Again, I nervously watched as she brought out the young horse and saddled her in the corral. The filly looked a bit skittish, but nothing more. Kathy mounted with assurance and rode easily around the confined space with no problem. It was good to see her so happy with the filly's performance, because I knew she had been secretly apprehensive.

Soon the outfit was on the move again for a tough 42-kilometre ride to the open meadows of the Banff airstrip and the end of the trip. I thought that the herd had settled down, resigned to returning to the parks for the summer work, but nothing is ever over until it's over. Repeatedly, small bunches of horses tried to escape, leading to some desperate riding at full gallop through the bush. The main herd had to keep moving, and it was tiring work rounding up the strays and pushing them hard to regain lost ground, but adrenaline was still running high as challenge after challenge presented itself. We also knew that once we hit the open flats before the barns in Banff, it would be a free-for-all as we tried to

Trailing horses near the Panther River

contain the stampede that would ensue.

I didn't know that the event had attracted the attention of the media and the public. When we reached the airstrip, a crowd had gathered to cheer on the arrival of the colourful horses. And what a spectacle it was! Over 120 horses thundered across the field with several wardens hot on their heels, following them to the waiting corrals. Cameras were flashing and I think people were yelling. All I remember was staying with the herd and keeping them going in the general direction of the barns. Way off to the left, Kathy was riding flat out on her colt, laughing with excitement. Everyone was. Suddenly, that moment in time nobody would ever forget was all over.

As we turned our horses loose and settled down, exhausted, to some beer and sandwiches, we knew the whole adventure had been a success. Reinforcements arrived to take care of the horses, now that they had come in, and parcelled them out to the respective parks. The absentee Earl was there to give Kathy a hand with the Yoho horses. There wasn't room for all the animals in the Banff barns, so each outfit was trucked the rest of the way to their summer home. That didn't leave much time for socializing; quick goodbyes were dashed off as horses were sorted and loaded. Everyone who knew the animals individually pitched in; no one wanted to take home the wrong horses. Johnny Nylund, who knew every horse's description by heart, supervised the whole thing closely.

Now on comfortable speaking terms with my wife, I wished her a good trip to Yoho and told her I would see her at home. We had had a major adventure together, one neither of us would forget. At least, I was quite sure she would never let *me* forget. I had made it very clear

I didn't want her along on the trip. It was obviously time I accepted women in the warden service — everyone else had.

Acknowledgments

The author would like to acknowledge the following individuals for their helpful contributions to the book: Dave Wildman, June Mickle, and Louis Kohler. In particular, I want to thank Donny Mickle, Bob Haney, and Perry Jacobson for their critical analysis of the stories and Donny's support and encouragement throughout the writing process. I also wish to thank Scott Ward for his generosity in allowing me to use his splendid poem, *Ya Ha Tinda Bound*, and finally I would like to thank my wife Kathy for her contributions to the book, her long standing support, and her editorial critique.

About the Author

Dale Portman is a retired park warden who spent 28 years with Parks Canada, often involved with back-country travel, mountain rescue, and avalanche control work in Jasper, Banff, Yoho, and Glacier/Revelstoke National Parks. He and his wife, Kathy, also a retired park warden, live in Calgary and head to the mountains as often as possible. Dale is currently assisting his wife Kathy, on a book, The Story of Mountain Rescue in the Canadian Rockies. His greatest love, besides traveling abroad, is for extended trips to the more remote parts of the Canadian Rockies, either by skis, on foot, or on horseback leading a packhorse or two.

Photo Credits

Cover: Comstock Images; Dale Portman collection: pages 19, 34 & 116; Donny Mickle: page 79.